BOUNDLESS
POTENTIAL

Also by Mark S. Walton

**Generating Buy-In: Mastering
the Language of Leadership**

BOUNDLESS

TRANSFORM YOUR BRAIN, UNLEASH YOUR TALENTS, REINVENT YOUR WORK IN MIDLIFE AND BEYOND

POTENTIAL

Mark S. Walton

New York Chicago San Francisco Lisbon London Madrid Mexico City
Milan New Delhi San Juan Seoul Singapore Sydney Toronto

1 2 3 4 5 6 7 8 9 10   DOC/DOC   1 9 8 7 6 5 4 3 2

ISBN: 978-0-07-178785-7
MHID: 0-07-178785-2

e-ISBN: 978-0-07-178786-4
e-MHID: 0-07-178786-0

Library of Congress Cataloging-in-Publication Data

Walton, Mark S.
  Boundless potential : transform your brain, unleash your talents, reinvent your work in midlife and beyond / by Mark S.Walton.— 1
    p. cm.
  Includes bibliographical references and index.
  ISBN-13: 978-0-07-178785-7 (hardback : acid-free paper)
  ISBN-10: 0-07-178785-2 (hardback : acid-free paper)
 1. Midlife crisis. 2. Vocational guidance. 3. Middle-aged persons. I. Title.
  BF724.65.M53W35 2012
  155.6'69—dc23

                                                        2011042208

McGraw-Hill books are available at special quantity discounts to use as premiums and sales promotions, or for use in corporate training programs. To contact a representative, please e-mail us at bulksales@mcgraw-hill.com.

This book is printed on acid-free paper.

To Jane with much love.
May our world fully realize
its boundless potential.
Pass it on.

Contents

part 3

HAPPINESS BUILT TO LAST

Thy life's a miracle.
Speak yet again.

—King Lear, IV, vi, 55

PART ONE

The Reinventive Process

chapter
one

The New Normal

Meeting on the Edge of Tomorrow

Change is the law of life.
And those who look only to the past or present are
certain to miss the future.
— John F. Kennedy

Nearly twenty-seven centuries ago, the Greeks invented the first reality show—sort of an "Olympic Idol" of the times.

Today, we know it as the *decathlon*.

Ten separate events over two grueling days, in competitive running, jumping, hurdling, shot put, pole vault, and javelin—tests designed to rip apart the body, mind, and soul through inherently contradictory demands: the need to gain strength without losing speed, conserve energy while extending distance, boost performance here without deteriorating elsewhere.

At the 1976 Olympic Games in Montreal, Bruce Jenner, the American contender, showed the world how the decathlon could be won. He not only took home the gold medal, but with 8,617 combined points, he also set a new record in this ancient

3

contest—an achievement that qualified him for the title "World's Greatest Athlete."

With global television audiences cheering him on, Bruce ran an impromptu victory lap around the field, gave his wife a congratulatory kiss, and, exiting the stadium, put down his vaulting poles for the last time.

"I always dreamed of winning the Games," said the champion, who had prepared relentlessly for this moment.

Yet the reality was more like a nightmare. As champagne corks popped in his honor that evening, Bruce sat alone in his hotel suite overlooking the Olympic city—and cried.

"It's like learning to play the piano. You sit in front of it for years, and you have a chance to play the most beautiful music in the world, and when it's over, you put your hands in your pockets and you never play that music again."

"I have no plans," he told an interviewer. "What will I do tomorrow?"

I've never run, let alone won, a decathlon. But I'm not sure we need to in order to see ourselves in Bruce's story.

We complete our degrees. We set out to develop an expertise; build a career; raise a family; start a practice, business, or organization. Over the years, and despite the odds, sacrifices, complexities, and competition, we achieve our objectives.

We taste our personal "Olympic" dreams.

Then, at some point—often when we least expect it—an unwelcome, even harrowing new uncertainty appears.

What Will I Do Tomorrow?

For some of us, the problem surfaces suddenly—the economy takes a hit; business conditions change; our jobs, homes, or investments are impacted; our future plans are disrupted or de-railed. "First it's shock, and then you get angry," said one pink-slipped 47-year-old executive, "and then you wonder, What am I going to do?"

For others, the doubts start bubbling up gradually. We find ourselves restless, dissatisfied and unchallenged at work. Or, having sampled the "retirement lifestyle," we feel trapped, disillusioned, and incomplete as we gaze at the road ahead.

What Now?

However the dilemma first arrives, it brings with it a set of concerns that grows disturbingly present and clear:

- Should I try to continue the kind of work I've done? Will I be able to? Is that what I really want anyway? Is it worth the effort to try?
- Maybe I should do something new. But what would it be? How hard would I have to work? How much money could I earn? Would I need to make an upfront investment? What if it doesn't pan out?
- Maybe I should just forget it. I'll kick back and relax. But what will I do with my time? How many years do I have ahead of me? How long will I be able to afford it?

With questions such as these in mind, I trust that you will appreciate what drove me to visit Aspen, Colorado, in the summer before my fifty-fifth birthday.

Despite their beauty, it was not the rocky mountain trails or luminescent rivers. Nor was it the splendid festivals or intense political dialogues at the famed Aspen Institute that I'd heard about for so many years.

It was a seminar there—something I'd normally have avoided at all costs on a glorious mid-July week like this one. But surfing the Internet a few days earlier, I'd stumbled on an entry in the institute's catalog that wouldn't let go of my psyche:

> ▶ PROFESSIONALS and businesspeople in midlife are increasingly asking themselves "What's Next?" in their careers and personal lives. The "Pursuing the Good Life" seminar draws on the wisdom of the ages to help practical men and women plan for satisfying, useful, and meaningful second halves.

At first, I was embarrassed to sign up, worried that I would feel out of place among younger people, tackling their early midlife crises.

I'd already been there and done that.

I started in radio news as a teenager. Straight out of college, I landed on the Washington, D.C., fast track, moving from press aide to the Secretary of the Navy, to CNN's chief White House correspondent by age 30, and soon after, to the position of network anchor and senior correspondent. I became a familiar face in the corridors of power and in millions of homes. I traveled the United States and the globe many times over and covered the biggest stories of the times.

In my early forties, I left the news business and reinvented myself, founding an executive development firm that attracted, as clients, some of the nation's leading graduate business schools and organizations.

I wrote a book on persuasive leadership that was named one of the top business books of the year.

Now in my mid-fifties, I was living, with my wife of three decades, in the town of our dreams on the coast of California. Our daughter was in graduate school on a fellowship that would lead to an excellent career. I could arrange my schedule to allow plenty of free time for running, hiking, travel, and friends.

I had health, liberty, good fortune, and a bit of fame—the gold medal of American life.

And I was increasingly unhappy: bored and irritable during the daytime, confused and conflicted as I lay awake at night.

What Should I Do with the Rest of My Life?

On arriving in Aspen, my biggest discovery was that, in this quandary, I was far from alone.

While some of my fellow seminarians were early forty-somethings, many were in their fifties and older: a highly respected investment banker, the CEO of a global workforce management firm, the former admissions director of a top private college, a superstar cancer surgeon, two accomplished entrepreneurs, and a managing partner of one of the world's premier consulting companies, to name a few.

Without exception, they were ambitious, intelligent, and accomplished people. They had loving relationships with spouses, children, and, in some cases, grandchildren. They were in no way regretful, disappointed, or malcontent about decisions they had made along the way.

Yet what drew them into a windowless meeting room on those picture perfect Aspen days were the same kinds of doubts and concerns that brought me:

After a career of 20, 30, or 40 years, am I a done deal?

Is it true that success is necessarily a younger person's game?

What will make me happiest now?

Have I had a positive impact on the world?

Where do I go from here?

In the group was a nationally known district attorney, thrown out of office in a brutal reelection campaign:

I worked hard since before I was a teenager. I was always go, go, go. I gave 32 years of my life to the law, to the district attorney's office, and to the criminal justice system. I'm absolutely convinced that I will live in good mental and physical health for another 30 years. Now I really want to do something else. But what should it be?

And from the former chief executive who, during his years in Washington, D.C., had built the most powerful advocacy force in American politics, there was this:

They had the retirement party, and one of the speakers was Newt Gingrich who said: "Well, you're 63. Now the game begins." And I thought to myself: You know, for most people the common mindset is, you stop working and you play golf, or go fishing, and then you die. Not me. The question I have is: Where are the things that I can have the biggest impact on, that will be the most meaningful? By God, people say, at 66 or 67, there's not much you can do. But for me, that's just plain crazy!

For four solid days, and as many wine-filled evenings, we exchanged experiences, hopes, philosophies, and dreams:

Is it possible to make money and a difference into our sixties, seventies, and beyond?

Might there be more potential within each of us than we've been led to believe?

Could living a long life have a greater purpose than most people think?

"To raise new questions marks real advance," wrote Albert Einstein.

And it was obvious, during our time and conversations together, that new ground had been broken, new perspectives gained.

But also unmistakably apparent—in more cases than not—was that many of our inquiries remained unsettled, our answers elusive or incomplete.

And as we said our goodbyes in Aspen, I decided on a personal course of action: I would not return to life as usual. Instead, I would make it my objective to research whatever, travel wherever, and find whoever could help me resolve these issues once and for all. I took on this project as though my future depended on it, which in fact I believe it does.

This book is the result.

If you have read this far, may I assume that you have arrived at a place in your own life where these matters are of importance to you, as well?

Or perhaps to someone you care about?

People You Will Meet in This Book

This book's pages contain the real-life experiences and pragmatic wisdom of uncommon men and women—people who have led the second half of their lives in an extraordinary way.

Each made a conscious choice to raise the bar, rather than lower his or her expectations. They decided to keep "going for the gold" in their way of living—to design and play a different game.

In midlife and beyond, they set out to reinvent their earlier success by creating a new kind of work they could truly love. And in doing so, they built a rich livelihood and legacy based on their full lifetime potential, not just the choices and necessities of earlier years.

As I encountered such people in the process of my research, I came to describe them as *reinventive*, and, by extension, to label the nature of their pursuits *reinventive work*.

"Why live on just one cylinder," one reinventive woman asked me, "never experiencing the joy and power of the rest?"

Meeting such individuals and, in particular, conducting the in-depth personal interviews that are an integral part of this book, has been a profoundly awakening experience for me, as I intend that reading the pages ahead will be for you.

Included are several people I initially encountered during my time in Aspen, but most are men and women I've come to know since.

Be assured, this is no volume of theory or chicken soup for growing older.

It is a practical inquiry into the challenges of today and tomorrow, an intelligent person's guide to a fundamentally new—a twenty-first-century—redefinition of the word *success*.

Life's NEW Second Half

Over the past century, two monumental changes powerfully converged to alter the course of our lives.

Our Life Expectancy Skyrocketed

When my father was born in 1917, the average life expectancy at birth in America was a little over 50 years. When my daughter was born in 1980, the expected life span was close to 75 years and still climbing.

As I write this today, those of us who cross the threshold of age 65 can expect to live, on average, into our mid-eighties. Many of us will make it into our nineties—perhaps beyond.

The experts have little trouble explaining these advances: the twentieth century produced continuing improvements in medicine, health care, sanitation, lifestyle, and diet. But the velocity and cumulative impact of all this was greater than anyone could have imagined.

In a matter of decades, we experienced an increase in longevity roughly equal to that which occurred over all the previous history of western civilization.[1]

What's more, at the same time this was occurring, other dramatic shifts were also under way.

The Nature of Our Economy and Work
Radically Changed

In the mid-twentieth century, following the mass introduction of silicon chips, smaller computers, and other new information technologies, the knowledge economy was born.

Where it had not happened earlier, the full spectrum of human work was transformed: whatever our jobs, professions, fields, or endeavors, almost all of us soon became *knowledge workers*, people who made our living on brainpower rather than brawn.

Even in the most muscular working environment—the factory floor—intelligence-based skills, creativity, and problem solving supplanted mind-numbing routine and brute force.

The combined benefits of our new longevity and knowledge economy are clear: longer, healthier lives in a richer, better-informed, and more closely connected world.

Less obvious, however, are the landmark challenges that these developments brought along: paradigm shifts for which few individuals or institutions were—or may yet be—fully prepared.

One man understood the implications of all of this, long before anyone else.

He was Peter F. Drucker, widely considered the father of modern management and the leading business futurist of our time.

In 1999, in his thirty-third major book, *Management Challenges for the 21st Century*, Drucker observed that, taken together, these changes and challenges constituted a total "revolution in human affairs."[2]

And he predicted that while this revolution would eventually affect everyone, its impact would most immediately be felt by those of us who are currently between our mid-forties and about 70 years old.

Why? Because, we are "the first age cohort in human history, a majority of which did not go into manual work but increasingly into knowledge work," a term Drucker originated in 1959.

We can expect to live longer than any population before us.

But due to the nature of our economy and work, we will also face a series of problems no previous generation has faced:

Some of us will lose our jobs and financial footing and have trouble affording our new, longer lives.

Some of us will remain employed but grow increasingly unchallenged.

Some of us will retire and feel like we're losing our minds.

Let's examine these scenarios one at a time.

SCENARIO 1. Some of Us Will Lose Our Jobs and Financial Footing and Have Trouble Affording Our New, Longer Lives

In today's knowledge-based economy, speed has replaced stability; and innovation has supplanted permanence. New technologies can reconfigure entire industries, and economic upheavals (think 2008 through 2009) can scale down or wipe out even the longest-lived organization, career plan, or retirement nest egg, seemingly overnight.

In such an environment, warned Drucker, relatively few of us can expect to avoid a serious, perhaps debilitating, personal setback at some point in midlife or beyond.

For one thing, whether we are employees or outside contractors, we knowledge workers are likely to outlast the organizations we work for. Though we may have developed a 40-year career plan, in the new economy, the life expectancy of the average organization can be considerably shorter than that. For another thing, even if the organizations we need are still around, they may no longer need us. Both commercial and nonprofit organizations may change their structure, the work they do, the knowledge they utilize, and the kinds of people they require, over and over again.

Scenario 2. Some of Us Will Remain Employed but Grow Increasingly Unchallenged

What if, despite the obstacles, we manage to hang in there? For many knowledge workers, this scenario can be nearly as bad as the first: the original work that was so challenging when we were in our thirties or early forties often becomes monotonous and unrewarding as time goes on. For financial reasons, we feel the need to persevere, but few of us are still learning anything. Drucker said, "Few are contributing anything more. They deteriorate, get bored, lose all joy in their work, retire on the job, and become a burden to themselves and everyone around."

Scenario 3. Some of Us Will Retire and Feel Like We're Losing Our Minds

If we knowledge workers finally do pack it in, the traditional "retirement lifestyle" may be the worst experience of all. Endless stretches of leisure can feel more like a death sentence than a blessing. Hobbies and travel are only temporary distractions. We have nothing pending to accomplish, nothing worth thinking about. We face a problem that can threaten not only our mental but our physical well-being: we don't want our brains to stop working, but we don't know what to do with them next.

These three potential scenarios—unemployment, underemployment, or an unfulfilling retirement—all lead to the same bottom line.

What's Next?

Peter Drucker—who was awarded the Presidential Medal of Freedom at age 93 and continued writing, teaching, and consulting actively until his death at 95—concluded that this question would inevitably affect almost all of us whose careers were based on the power of our minds.

Yesteryear's manual workers, he wrote, who had spent "forty years in the steel mill for instance, or the cab of a locomotive" were physically used up—they were "finished." If they survived, they were "quite happy" to spend their few remaining years "doing nothing, playing golf, going fishing, engaging in some minor hobby and so on."

But for people who work with their brains, the old paradigm no longer applies.

Why? Because knowledge workers are never truly finished or worn out.

Moreover, with the gift of our longevity, most of us will be capable of extending our achievements for decades to come.

"This creates a totally new challenge," counseled Drucker.

What to Do with the NEW Second Half of Life?

We cannot cling to the past, Drucker advised; we must open our minds to new ideas, to experiment with and profit from the fresh challenges we face.

Those of us who fully rise to this occasion may be "a uniquely ambitious few," said the visionary leader. But it will be this group, "those who see the long working-life expectancy as an opportunity both for themselves and for society, who may increasingly become the leaders and the models, . . . the success stories of the future."

It is precisely such individuals you will meet in the pages to come—intelligent men and women who encountered the obstacles and setbacks, only to move forward and *act on the inquiry*:

If Life Has Changed, How Do I Reinvent the Game?

What are such people like? How did they get started? What did they accomplish? What new talents or powers did they discover? What advice do they have for the rest of us? Is there some common strategy they followed? How can we use their experience for ourselves?

That's what the case studies—the success stories—in this book are about.

Ahead are firsthand accounts of people who leveraged their earlier accomplishments, as well as discovered within themselves previously unrecognized capabilities, to create new profits, lasting happiness, and a huge positive impact—from midlife well into their seventies, eighties, and even nineties.

Throughout the pages to come we'll hear from such people directly, as though they were personal mentors or friends.

- In Part 1, "The Reinventive Process," we'll learn their methodology and the action steps they took to change the course of their lives and work.

- In Part 2, "The Science of Lifelong Success," we'll explore the emerging neuroscience of lifelong potential: revolutionary new discoveries about the unique intellectual and creative powers that become available to each of us exclusively in midlife and beyond.

- In Part 3, "Happiness Built to Last," we'll see how "paying it forward," generating a legacy for future generations, can pay us back with unexpected gifts of long-term happiness and health. And we'll take a no-nonsense look at the ways in which audacity, smart planning, and "just plain luck" can converge to create a second half of life that's even better than the first.

This is a book for people facing life's new challenges, people who are motivated—by the desire, need, or the influence of both—to realize their boundless potential.

chapter two

Where Is Your Fascination?

Success Story: Sherwin B. Nuland

Whatever you can do, or dream you can, begin it.
— Johann Wolfgang von Goethe

Had you traveled with me to a certain Connecticut village, climbed the staircase of a particular rambling white house, and leaned against the door of the sun-filled study on the second floor, you would have found retired surgeon Sherwin B. Nuland sitting with his back to you in a big comfortable chair.

Observing quietly for a moment, you could easily have mistaken the slight, intermittent movements of his head and shoulders for the involuntary quivers of a midmorning nap.

But from the other side of "Shep" Nuland's heavy oak desk, the picture would have looked quite different: between his fingers was a yellow no. 2 Eberhard pencil, moving deliberately across a long white legal pad.

Most likely you would not have recognized this as a state of peak performance, the kind that behavioral psychologists who study athletes, soldiers, software designers, stock traders, and ballet dancers see all the time.

They call it being "in the zone" or, more simply, "in the *flow*," a shorthand for the optimal human experience, a scientifically measurable condition in which perception is altered and otherwise unattainable achievements become possible.

Flow is often defined as a unique dimension in which skills and challenges face off and the most demanding work becomes a game. Not exactly the kind of place you'd expect to find a late 70-something-year-old.

But after decades of high accomplishment in the operating room, Dr. Nuland had found a new domain in which to play.

How to describe Shep when I first met him? The kind of surgeon to whom I'd comfortably trust my life. His handshake was firm but gently assuring. His voice, soft yet easily understood. His eyes were confident and disarmingly compassionate.

"Am I retired?" he asked rhetorically, as we sat down in front of a fireplace that added a welcome notch of warmth to the New England chill in the room.

After a moment, Shep went on to address his own inquiry:

> *Well, you'd have to define your terms. The classical definition of a "retiree" is someone who goes out and puts on white shoes and starts playing shuffleboard in Miami. I've "retired" from doing clinical surgery, yes. But have I retired in that other way? Absolutely not. I hope that never happens. What I've done is make a lateral arabesque into something that I'm enjoying immensely and seems to have no end in sight.*

I had flown across the country to see him because of the remarkable occurrence in his life, some 14 years before. Suddenly and unpredictably, Shep had discovered that, in addition to being a distinguished physician, professor, and scholar of medical history at Yale, he'd become a bestselling author, as well:

> *I was overwhelmed by it, Mark. You can't imagine what happened. One day nobody knows you, and the next day you're on the TODAY show and Charlie Rose. And the next day you're in a hotel somewhere in Washington, talking on two phones at the same time because everybody wants you. You know, I'm an obsessional surgeon. But there's no way to think clearly about how to handle what's happening in your life.*

What happened was the publication of his book *How We Die: Reflections on Life's Final Chapter*, an unprecedented and highly detailed journey into an area that legions of other writers—and readers—had diligently avoided.

Shep, increasingly conscious of his own mortality as he entered his sixties and feeling a keen desire to extend the benefits of his experience beyond the reach of the scalpel's blade, wrote this:

> *This is the book in which I will try to tell what I have learned. . . . By trooping some of the army of the horsemen of death across the field of our vision, I hope to recall things I have seen, and make them familiar to everyone else. Perhaps these horsemen will also become less frightening.*[1]

The reaction was magnetic: *How We Die* won the National Book Award for Nonfiction, remained on the *New York Times'* bestseller list for 34 weeks, was translated into 17 languages, and was named a Pulitzer Prize finalist.

It was the book that launched a whole new genre of popular literature—the in-depth medical memoir by a real-life, practicing surgeon.

None of this, mind you, was the fruit of any long-conscious dream or ambition. What happened to the good doctor at age 64 was as much a shock to him as anyone else. Looking back, however, you can see the seeds of Shep's reinvention in the DNA of his early life.

Born to immigrants Meyer and Vitsche Nudelman, Shep was raised by his grandmother and aunt among the Old World Jews, Italians, and Irish in the Bronx, the northernmost borough of New York City:

> I came from a home where English was a second language. People like us have a love for this language. Born in this immigrant enclave, the language, the ability to speak it, to write it, this was how I was going to find America, which didn't exist in the Bronx of the 1930s. So English became my key, not just to liberation but to understanding society and becoming part of it.

But for young Shep there was still something more—a special fascination with the way language could be used to describe and share experiences of the strange new world around him:

> Conversation, I loved conversation. Every Friday evening people would come by trolley, by subway, by walking, and sit around the living room and tell stories! And I would sit and listen to those stories.
>
> I remember when I was about eight years old, there was a carnival on a vacant lot. I'd never seen anything like this. I

went by myself, and I saw these rides and pitching pennies and who knows what. And I just had to write about it! I came running home, and we were not a family where writing paper was around. But someone had given me this little book, and the front and back flaps were empty, white sheets. So I took a pencil and wrote, as fast as I could, my description of this.

And one day, seven or eight years ago, I found it again. I'd kept this in my library to remind me, that's what I began doing at the age of eight—telling stories, having conversations.

And how well I remember applying to medical school in 1950, and one of the common standard questions on interviews was, what are your hobbies? And I would say, storytelling is one of my hobbies. And I would always get this sort of look!

Let me make sure I understand this, I said to him, somewhat anxiously, as I shifted position in my seat: you loved telling and writing stories as a kid. And during your surgical career, of course you wrote the usual medical articles and papers. But the first time you tried writing for a general audience, you were already in your fifties? And a few years later you turned out this huge bestseller?

How could this possibly happen?

Well, I was at the height of a busy surgical career, and there was a man who was starting a program of reprinting classics in medicine, some of the great books. He wanted someone to write essays about each of these books, and he asked me because of my interest in medical history and perhaps my interest in writing.

And so I discovered myself explaining things to someone who didn't know the medical history that I knew. Perhaps someone who had been an engineer or a school teacher but who had the same kind of curiosity that I did, who wanted to know the kinds of things that interested me but didn't have the technical knowledge I had. So I found myself explaining it to her, or to him, in a way that makes sense in an ordinary conversation.

This unforeseen turn of events led Shep to try his hand at a book of medical biographies, and several years later, to schedule a sabbatical from the professional treadmill, at a time when he felt "the joy of being a surgeon" begin to fade.

It was during this hiatus, from which he never returned, that Shep designed a challenge for himself and his newly developing skills: a second half of life experiment that would become *How We Die*:

The symmetry of the thing was remarkable to me, Mark. When I first started working on the book, I was thinking in terms of, and here's an interesting word, of an assignment. I had assigned myself that here was an area in which I had to enlighten that reader.

I would do it just like a surgical operation. I would divide it into aspects of the problem. Like, you open the skin, you open the abdomen, you expose the organs, dissect the organs, remove whatever you're removing, you put it together, then you begin to close.

I started writing on the morning of January 2, 1992, and I finished writing on the morning of January 2, 1993. I was exactly 63. I sat down with a pencil and pad, and I just let it happen. I stopped when I got tired at one or two in the afternoon, and I just picked up again the next day.

And lo and behold, my unconscious gave me a beginning, middle, and an end. And it also enabled me to express a lot of stuff that was inside of me, that had been a determinant of my behavior and my thinking, that I didn't even know existed.

About two weeks before it was due to be published, my editor called me. And he was a young guy in his middle thirties. And, you know, I was over 60 at the time. And he said, "Shep, you better read your book."

And I said, "That's the dumbest thing a smart guy could say to me." And he said, "Please just do me a favor and read your book." I said, "I've just read the galleys six times." "No, No, No," he said. "Sit down like you've never read it before."

Well, it took me more than a week to read that book, because I would become emotional with each paragraph. I saw things that I couldn't remember having written. I saw a philosophy that I had obviously been living by but I had not been consciously aware of.

I was flabbergasted by this! God, . . . did you write this? Did you write this? And then, of course, I thought back on my experience of taking care of sick people and realized, of course, who else could have done it?

I first heard about Shep from a mutual friend who knew I was on the lookout for people who had done interesting things with what are traditionally the "retirement" years. But my friend hadn't related the entirety of Shep's story.

In retrospect, I think he wanted me to hear it firsthand.

Everything about Shep—the emergence of this remarkable talent in his early fifties, the joy, success, significance, and notoriety that accompanied it—flew in the face of conventional thinking, of how our lives are supposed to be.

It directly contradicted what we've long been led to accept about growing older: that our potential is fundamentally depleted, that our capacities for further accomplishment are diminished, that the "flow" of creativity and achievement—the joie de vivre for successful people—is something we can no longer aspire to.

As one observer put it, "Ever since the industrial age, career tracks have been built on the assumption that you can work around the clock in your twenties, shoulder increasing responsibility in your thirties and forties, and begin to ratchet down and move over for the next generation in your fifties and sixties."[2]

Try telling that to Shep Nuland.

By the time of my visit with him, just short of his seventy-eighth birthday, he had become a one-man literary phenomenon, authoring seven additional books, all released by major publishers. This, plus numerous articles in the *New York Times*, the *New Yorker*, *Time* magazine, *American Scholar*, *National Geographic*, and the *New Republic*, as well as speaking engagements at major conferences and frequent appearances on NPR and PBS.

This was not the model of life's second half that I had been raised to expect.

My parents and their parents before them had done pretty much the same thing. They'd worked hard, raised families, and when they hit their late fifties or early sixties, they took whatever money they had and retired, for better or worse.

That idea didn't appeal to Shep Nuland in the least:

No, I've never been interested in doing something that I know would be the most boring thing I've ever done. Because this is what so often happens: you get some high-powered person who says, "Oh my God, I can't wait until they give me that gold watch, and I can go play golf." And the person finds out later that this is not what he or she really wanted.

You see it particularly among professionals. Many people seem to identify with their careers or occupations. They're doctors—that's all they are. Or they're engineers—that's it. And then one day, it's over! Suddenly they've lost their identity, and they've lost the thing that gives them stature in their own eyes and the stature they see reflected in the eyes of other people. And they become useless to themselves.

Why is the idea of retirement still so powerful? I think because people look forward to it for so many years. But they don't know until they get into it that it's distorted their lives and sent them off on a tangent that is not the continuation of what they have always been.

Someday, someone is going to study coronary rates among people within a year after retirement. And they're going to find the predictable thing, that they're higher than they were in the previous five-year period. Or they're higher in people who retire to that sunbelt of expectations with their "go to hell" pants and play golf or shuffleboard or whatever it is.

As we sat together, I wondered out loud: Did he perceive some underlying purpose to the second half of life? Something the rest of us might not be aware of?

Absolutely. The purpose is to continue to develop your real humanity. I think our real humanity often gets stunted by our occupational years.

You come out of college, and you begin working for some big company, and everything that has come before is laid aside. You become an executive, a stockbroker, a doctor, a lawyer, or whatever, and all of your energies are devoted to that. And you become something less than your full potential.

Unlike most other animals, the human species lives long beyond its reproductive years, and it is the only animal with the ability to continue developing in these later stages of life. I think we should consider that a gift.

The years of midlife and beyond are simply a new developmental period. The key word here is "developmental." You have to look for something that is in continuity with the previous 10, 15, 20 years of your life. That choice exists for each of us.

I recall my mind racing back and forth at this point in our exchange. I wanted to continue talking. Yet at the same time, I felt the need to sit quietly for a moment, just to hear myself think.

Shep didn't seem to care. In fact, I think he understood. On a gut level, I knew what he was saying made sense. And the way he was leading his own life seemed proof absolute.

But in preparing to write this book, I had researched much of the professional literature on human development. Almost all of it emphasized the first half of life—especially childhood and adolescence.[3] "Adult development is still a mystery," however, wrote pioneering researcher George Valliant of Harvard in 2002, "and, as a field for scientific study, very new."[4]

Among the big-name sages of the twentieth century, even the basic notion that we might continue developing throughout life was vigorously pooh-poohed.

Sigmund Freud, the godfather of modern psychology, was adamant that by age 30, at the latest, human development was a done deal. By 50, according to Freud, "the elasticity of the mental process is as a rule lacking. . . . People are no longer educable."[5] Cognitive development pioneer Jean Piaget believed pretty much the same thing, despite the fact that he personally continued publishing until his death at age 84.[6]

And when questioned during a seminar about the possibility of continued growth past midlife, the great behavioral psychologist B. F. Skinner became livid, according to one participant. Age and growth, Skinner asserted, were a contradiction in terms.[7]

Only a few exceptional thinkers—psychologists Erik Erikson and Carl Jung in particular—gave much credence to the proposition that life's second half was a fertile period for personal development.

But neither of them saw or described it quite like Sherwin B. Nuland did:

Crazy idea? I think the crazy idea is the kind of unnatural discontinuity that people subject themselves to. Our culture has created that thing. But that's not what's natural in us. What's natural in us is to continue our development.

Every stage of your life has been prepared for by everything that came before it. It's just a simple matter of natural growth to me. One of our biggest problems is the preconception we learned from previous generations. They passed down the idea that there are epics in life—youth, career, retirement, and so forth.

So we now have expectations of what certain phases of our lives should be like that come from what we've seen in our parents and our grandparents. But that doesn't mean they're natural. They're societal. We've structured them this way.

My argument is that it's the gradual continuity of life that's natural. Knowledge is like a tree. The longer you live and the more you've thought about things, the more branches there are and the more possibilities you have. We don't lose creativity until our eyes are closed by the minister or the doctor even if it's at age 101.

Why throw that away?

When my tape recorder clicked off, signaling that I needed to switch cassettes again, I looked down at my watch. We'd been together for nearly two hours. The more deeply I had listened to Shep, the more I'd become absorbed in his point of view. In fact, it was nearly contagious.

But now was the time to get real. My goal for this book was more than philosophy. My objective was to draw a practical map for this road less taken, an actionable life design for others to follow—to make the second half of life as joyful, purposeful, and successful as the first.

What's required for this kind of living? Where exactly does one start?

I think when you get into your mid- to late forties, fifties, or early sixties—and this was my experience—you should start to look back, begin to rediscover who you were when you were 15, 25, or 30 with all that wide range of things that fascinated you that you gave up to become a doctor, lawyer, engineer, business executive, and so forth, to care for a family or whatever.

You ask yourself: What most fascinates or interests me?

What's most rewarding for me? Where can I make a contribution? There should be this interest you begin to build so that when you stop the profession or activities with which you identify, you are just very easily coasting into this other thing that fascinates you.

You should begin looking for those things within yourself and expand the horizons of possibility. Then as you're getting older, you begin to bring those horizons into focus. You ask yourself: What can I actually do with this thing as the opportunities arise?

It doesn't happen right away. But over a period of months and years, you're gathering knowledge of this thing that fascinates you into this big ball, and you come to understand it. You just take it bit by bit with this thing that interests you so much that you're magnetized to it. And that's the way I've done it.

For me, it's my fascination with writing, storytelling, and what we call the "human condition." I'm trying to find out why we do the things we do—how we live, how we die.

For you, it will be something else. First you need to discover or rediscover what your fascination is. Then, you need to take it on, to put that thing to work. It's your project, really. It's the project for the rest of your life.

The sounds and smells of dinner cooking drifted up from the floor below. I felt guilty for possibly overstaying my welcome, but, to that point in my research, I'd never met anyone quite like Shep Nuland. And there were still things I needed to know: What was his next project? Were there ever moments when he found himself thinking, "It's time for a break"?

Yeah, I say it all the time, but I know I'm never gonna do it. I just wanna be better and better at everything I do. There's good old Dr. Freud who says the biggest things in life are work and love. With love you see yourself reflected in the eyes of someone else as a person of real value. With work, there's a product and the product is growth. It isn't always a visible product, but because it's accomplishment, it's growth within yourself.

When do I begin my next assignment? Right away. That's the way it has to be.

It's funny, because right now is the first time I've been in any kind of limbo for years. I got a call to review a book that I ordinarily would not have done, because of the nature of the book, but I said, absolutely. Because I just have to get to work until I begin my next book.

Actually, the contract I have next is a two-book contract. I've already completed the first book, which will come out next spring.

When that first book, *The Uncertain Art*, was published, the *New York Times* called it "a delightful companionable collection" of essays that "undermine the smug uncertainties of modern science."[8]

Meticulously intelligent and irreverent, like its author, it included Shep's trek to China to investigate the use of acupuncture in conjunction with modern surgery, a chapter on the effectiveness of placebo drugs, and a look at the mystery of electroshock therapy: why doctors use it to fight depression without being certain how it works.

A year later, as promised, the second book in Shep's contract, *The Soul of Medicine: Tales from the Bedside*, was released.

As I thanked him for our conversation and headed out into the late afternoon traffic, I turned back one last time. Could Shep ever foresee a moment, I asked, when he'd consider his fascination, his storytelling, complete?

It will go on and remain unfinished. Somewhere in How We Die, *I say we should never die with our work finished because with our work finished, that would imply that we had stopped, that we had not continued to grow.*

Somehow, I knew he would say that.

A Blueprint
for Reinvention

The Secret of Reinventive Work

After the White House,
what is there to do but drink?
— Franklin Pierce, 14th President
of the United States

Before I set out to write this book, had friends or colleagues tried to persuade me that the ultimate reward for years of hard work, the true key to everlasting happiness was . . . well, more work, I would have thought they were deranged.

After years of office politics, deadlines, budgets, and clients, after sacrificing, saving, investing, obsessing, and delaying gratifications, what possible sense could it make — if retirement was feasible — to go find, let alone invent, something new to work at?

Yet as I met and studied reinventive people like Shep Nuland — men and women who were successful and happy well into life's second half — I often thought of my grandfather, founder of one of America's first nationwide clothing chains.

I still have vivid boyhood memories of workday breakfasts with him at his home on the south shore of Long Island. "Buddy," as I called him, would come downstairs, cheerful and resplendent in a crisp white shirt and beautiful new tie, the scent of French aftershave around him.

After fresh-brewed coffee and a toasted corn muffin, he'd rise and declare: "So long, sweetheart," put on his suit coat, and head off for his Manhattan office, or for Grand Central Station and another coast-to-coast rail tour of his stores.

Then one morning, he came to the table in an outfit usually reserved for weekends: slacks and a sports shirt with a pocketful of Cuban cigars. He had followed the bylaws of his own corporation—in his early sixties he had retired.

At first, he seemed to relish his new life, filling the days with golf, card games, and lunch at the club. He crossed the Atlantic with my grandmother numerous times, sampling the best hotels and restaurants that London and Paris had to offer. He wintered in the Florida sunshine. He had four grown children, seven grandchildren, and several hobbies.

To outsiders, his postcareer years would indeed have appeared golden.

But, under the radar, our family noticed a strikingly different Buddy emerge. We watched a big man whose interests shrank, whose patience shortened, whose conversations and concerns turned trivial: train schedules, family hygiene, parking his Cadillac. For several decades after leaving the office, his body remained healthy and his memory sharp. But his life devolved— from full and interesting to small and pedantic.

At the time, of course, I didn't understand. But now, nearing Buddy's retirement age myself, and having the benefit of my research for this book, I do.

Though he possessed, and did, all the things you're supposed to in a so-called active retirement, he was bored, nearly out of his mind. Ironically, the fact that he could afford to permanently "kick back" was a big part of the problem.

Like Shep Nuland, he had been a knowledge worker—someone who had used his intelligence to achieve big things. But now he had nothing worth thinking about—nothing that fascinated or challenged him.

He had no avenue for further growth or development.

After designing his earlier years around accomplishment, he had failed to find what Shep and the other successful people in this book discovered in midlife and beyond: the joy, power, and purpose of what I have come to call *reinventive work*.

Reinventive Work

Reinventive work consists of self-created endeavors that unlock our unique lifetime potential, provide the highest levels of happiness, and have a meaningful impact in the world.

Depending on our wants and needs, such work can range from highly lucrative to fully altruistic, can be accomplished full or part-time, alone or within a group or organization.

Reinventive work has been a hallmark of the highest-functioning individuals since the dawn of western civilization.

No matter whether we find ourselves unemployed, underemployed, or retired and unchallenged, it is precisely this kind of work that Peter Drucker, the management visionary we discussed earlier, considered the principal means of ongoing happiness and achievement in midlife and beyond.

The Key to Successful Reinvention

In writings labeled "landmarks" by the *Harvard Business Review*, Drucker asserted that in the twenty-first century, "one can no longer expect that the organization for which one works" or, given ongoing changes in technology, that the work itself "will still be around." And even if it is, decades "in the same work is too long for most people."[1]

Thus, he said, extending one's success beyond the first half of life will require "that the knowledge worker develop a *second major interest*" and *create his or her own work based on this interest*. Should no organization be willing, or exist, to sponsor such work—which may well be the case—one must also be prepared to create that structure or organization.

In this post-industrial information age, Drucker advised, we will need to *manage ourselves*.

As mentioned previously, Peter Drucker had an unusual degree of personal insight into the topic.

After completing the manuscripts in which these thoughts initially appeared in 1999, he continued writing, lecturing, and working actively as a consultant to corporations and nonprofits, until his death, five years later, at age 95.

The Design of Reinvention

So, how do we go about designing our own reinventive work? The kind of work that will sustain us, profitably and happily, in the second half of our own lives?

Is there a certain kind of person we need to be?

In five years of researching these questions, here's what I discovered: reinventive people come from every imaginable background; their education, interests, previous careers, personalities, skills, and financial circumstances differ widely.

Yet for all their dissimilarities, there's an unmistakable pattern in the way they go about their reinventive process—a set of shared "best practices" that any of us can follow.

Later, we'll continue our in-depth visits with reinventive people.

But first let's explore the methodology they have in common and how you and I can put it to work for ourselves.

This process involves three sequential inquiries (steps)—and subsequent decisions—as outlined in Figure 3-1 and explained, in greater detail, in the remainder of this chapter and the next. (Steps 1 and 2 are covered in this chapter; Step 3 is covered in the next chapter.)

Step 1. Discover Your Fascination (Ask: What Is the Direction That Pulls Me Forward?)

When I first asked Shep Nuland where the journey to reinvention begins, he urged each of us to look into areas that we may have "given up to become a doctor, lawyer, engineer, business executive, and so forth, to care for a family or whatever" earlier in our lives.

Look to our *fascination*, he suggested.

Interestingly, the word *fascination* stems from the Latin word *fascinum*, which translates to mean "spell, charm, or enchantment." But what part does this play in midlife and beyond?

The Design of Reinvention

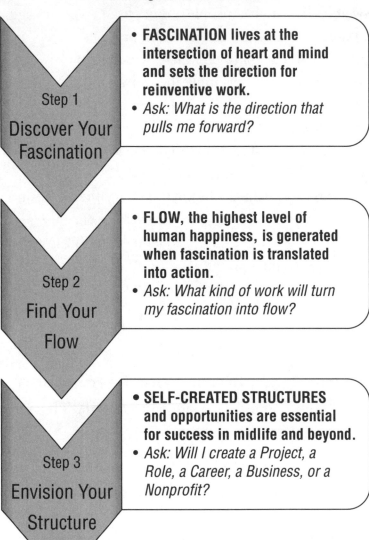

Step 1
Discover Your
Fascination

- **FASCINATION** lives at the intersection of heart and mind and sets the direction for reinventive work.
- *Ask: What is the direction that pulls me forward?*

Step 2
Find Your
Flow

- **FLOW, the highest level of human happiness, is generated when fascination is translated into action.**
- *Ask: What kind of work will turn my fascination into flow?*

Step 3
Envision Your
Structure

- **SELF-CREATED STRUCTURES and opportunities are essential for success in midlife and beyond.**
- *Ask: Will I create a Project, a Role, a Career, a Business, or a Nonprofit?*

Figure 3-1

What Role Does Fascination Have in Reinvention?

Actor and writer Ian Roberts has answered this way: "The world will probably get by without the product of your efforts." But that is not the point, he said. "The point is what the inner process of following your creative impulses will do to you. *Your fascination will pull your attention forward.*"[2]

Shep's fascination with storytelling pulled him forward into unpredictable achievements.

And with every reinventive man and woman I interviewed in writing this book, the process was much the same—some fascination pulled them forward, from what might otherwise have been an ordinary existence into an unanticipated and extraordinary new way of life.

Where Do You Locate Your Own Fascination?

Some time back, I ran across a column in the *Wall Street Journal* that points to an essential clue.

It tells the story of Paul Charron, who stepped down, after 12 years as chief executive of Liz Claiborne, the big apparel firm, at age 65.

Charron had grown weary of satisfying investors and directors and was seeking a way to fulfill his own needs. "I still want to work—but I don't miss being in my car at 5:30 every morning and having a headache by 6:30," he said.[3]

The only thing Charron knew for certain was what he did not want: He did not want to run another public company. He did not want to play golf. He did not want to devote all his time to charity work. And, while he'd done some teaching and enjoyed it, becoming a full-time professor was not something that interested him.

Eight months into retirement he was still searching, as he put it, "for the signal where my heart and head come together and I know . . . this is what I should do."

Charron was on the right track.

> *Fascination lives at the intersection of heart and mind.*
> *Fascination sets the direction for reinventive work.*

Based on my study of people who've successfully reinvented their work, fascination is frequently not a specific thing but rather a *sense of direction* toward an area of intrinsic interest to both heart and mind.

Hence the initial question to ask ourselves becomes: Where is my fascination?

What Pulls Your Attention Forward?

In the sense that we are using it, our fascination might have been called our "bliss" by the noted scholar of mythology Joseph Campbell.

Discovering and following one's bliss, according to Campbell, is a classic theme in the odyssey of human life. It centers on the "hero's journey" and his or her willingness to face down the "dragons"—metaphorical and otherwise—that inevitably appear on the road to success.

This was a philosophy of powerful living that Campbell taught at Sarah Lawrence University and shared with millions of viewers in highly acclaimed PBS television interviews conducted by journalist Bill Moyers:

Campbell: You may have success in life, but then just think of it—what kind of life was it? What good was it if you've never done the thing you wanted to do? The thing to do is bring life to it, and the only way to do that is to find, in your own case, where the life is and become alive. What is it that makes you happy? Stay with it no matter what people tell you. This is what I call "following your bliss."

Moyers: Are you saying that we should follow our bliss, follow our love, wherever it leads?

Campbell: Well, you've got to use your head. They say, you know, a narrow path is a very dangerous path—the razor's edge.

Moyers: So the heart and head should not be at war?

Campbell: No, they should not. They should be in cooperation. The head should be present, and the heart should listen to it now and then.

Moyers: Are there times when the heart is in the lead?

Campbell: That would be the desirable situation most of the time.[4]

A number of these interviews were recorded at Skywalker Ranch in California, owned by movie producer George Lucas, whose films—the Star Wars series in particular—were greatly influenced by Campbell's work. At Lucas's invitation, Campbell and Moyers sat down to view the "perils and heroics" of the films' hero, Luke Skywalker, and to discuss their meaning in all of our lives:

Moyers: How do I slay the dragon in me? What's the journey each of us has to make, what you call "the soul's high adventure"?

Campbell: Follow your bliss. *Find it where it is, and don't be afraid to follow it. If the work that you're doing is the work that you choose to do because you are enjoying it, that's it. But if you think: "Oh no! I couldn't do that!" that's the dragon locking you in.*[5]

Dragons and Dark Woods

What then, are our dragons—the obstacles that may confront us on the path to discovering our fascination and launching our new self-created work?

According to my research on reinventive people, the following three challenges are those most commonly encountered.

Challenge 1. Impatience

Successful men and women, by our very nature, are impatient individuals. We've been trained, since childhood, to target our goals and to move forward quickly and strategically, lest someone beat us to them. After years of having to make quick decisions under pressure, most of us suffer from something akin to a chronic attention deficit disorder. But patience and willingness to tolerate ambiguity are essential to uncovering our fascination. This is no Internet search. It is an internal venture.

Challenge 2. Inexperience with Introspection

Americans, especially, are outwardly oriented. We generally believe that the pursuit of happiness requires a concerted, often vigorous face-off with forces in the external world. Extroversion is often required later in the process of reinvention. To begin with, however, we need to develop different kinds of muscles: self-examination, deep inquiry, and imagination.

Challenge 3. Strongly Established Identity

After being a "grown-up" for 20 or 30 years, there is a certain "tranquilized obviousness" to our lives, to who we "hold ourselves" to be. We have become, in many ways, what we print on our business cards, what we put down on our tax forms. We are mothers, fathers, executives, doctors, lawyers, editors, accountants, scientists, educators, and so on.

Psychologists call this our "institutional identity." It took us a long time to develop these roles for ourselves, and if we have been successful, they have served us quite well. But in the same way that our professional identities are attached to us, for better and worse, we become glued to them.

Recognizing our fascination necessitates looking behind the labels we have adopted, penetrating our own PR. As Columbia University professor Joan Konner, executive producer of the Campbell-Moyers interviews, put it: "We are so engaged in activities of outer value, the pursuit of financial security and social gain . . . that we have little validation of our inner life, our souls. We lose touch with our inner sense of being that directs us toward those things that are most meaningful in our lives."[6]

There's No Perfect Strategy

Another thing I know about successful people: we tend to be perfectionists. It comes with the territory. For years, I have taught high-level executives precise leadership strategies to accelerate their business achievements.

Most take on my assignments like the Type A personalities I know them to be: they want to master "the system," including the type and timing of the results it will yield. Given the nature of the challenges before them, they are right to expect no less.

But in the quest for our fascination, this I can tell you with certainty: there is no one-size-fits-all strategy and no certain way to predict the schedule on which our fascination may emerge, the form it will take, or exactly where it will lead us:

Some people reaffirm a fascination from the past,

Some are compelled by an interest in the future,

Others discover something in between.

Clint Eastwood: Reaffirm and Innovate

For some people, especially "professional creatives" like artists, musicians, writers, or performers, the search for fascination can be a relatively short, circuitous trip. All the while struggling within the tedium of their existing work or the rigidity of their current identities, they manage to "fall in love again" with the original bliss that led them to where they are, while innovating new ways to explore and express it.

Clint Eastwood, the actor turned director, exemplifies this breed. Feeling constrained and stereotyped by the "Dirty Harry" tough guy roles that made him famous, Eastwood grew fascinated with other possibilities within his craft. Although his early attempts at directing met with less-than-stellar reviews, he continued on—through his sixties and well into his seventies—to win multiple Academy Awards as director, producer, and musical composer for numerous, surprisingly sensitive films.

Just prior to his eightieth birthday, Eastwood told an interviewer, "My dad was always talking about retiring and sitting next to a stream with a couple of beers in his hand. But retirement is not for me. The reason I don't retire is that I learn something new every day."[7] In another interview, he said, "You always have to learn, stretch your brain, experiment."[8]

Bill Gates: Reboot and Refocus

For entrepreneurs and experienced innovators, the search for fascination—and reinventive fulfillment—can be a variation on this theme.

"Not a retirement, a reordering of priorities," was how Bill Gates described his decision to leave his day-to-day role at Microsoft in 2008 and focus full-time on the foundation that he and his wife, Melinda, started a decade earlier. In making this shift, at age 52, Gates effectively redirected the fascinations at the core of his extraordinary early success to several growing interests and needs: health and development in the poorest countries and education in the United States.

Six months after the big changeover, Gates reported that his fascinations had successfully transferred: "My job at Microsoft had three magical things. First, there was the opportunity for big breakthroughs. Second, my skills would let me create a special company that would be part of a whole new industry. Finally, the work let me engage with people who were smart and knew things I didn't."

"I took a few weeks off, some for family time," said Gates, "but I was anxious to keep myself mentally challenged, and so the pause between jobs was brief. Many of my friends were concerned that I wouldn't find the foundation work as engaging or rewarding as my work at Microsoft. Despite that high bar, I love the work at the foundation. Although there are many differences, it also has the three magical elements."[9]

Marion Rosen: Rediscover and Reinvent

For others, however, the journey can prove more complex. This is particularly true of people who, for one reason or another, find themselves with little choice but to disengage from a career or way of life that they've known for many years.

A friend, for example, told me about meeting the ex-CEO of a major international bank, a 55-year-old who'd been forced out of his job as the result of a corporate merger. Said the former banker: "I used to be in *Who's Who*. Now even I don't know who I am."

For those of us mired in a predicament such as this, daily living can feel like a passage through Dante's *Inferno*:

> Midway in our life's journey, I went astray
> from the straight road and woke to find myself
> alone in a dark wood.
>
> Death could scarce be more bitter than that place,
> but since it came to good, I will recount all that
> I found revealed there by God's grace.[10]

But ironically, as in Dante's experience, this "dark wood" is frequently the very place where fascination—our "good"—actually reveals itself. For, as writer William Bridges has noted, "our most important beginnings take place in the darkness outside our awareness. First there is an ending, then a beginning, with an important empty or fallow time in between. That is the order of things in nature."

"You may feel this is heavy stuff," writes Bridges, who has long been a student of human change. But while in transition, the key thing to understand is this: "The way out is the way in; . . . when the wheels spin in loose gravel, you need more weight."[11]

Later in this book we will visit, in-depth, with several people who braved the dark wood as long as was necessary to gain the traction required for significant new success in life's second half.

Among them is Marion Rosen, who escaped Nazi Germany in her mid-twenties to settle in Berkeley, California, where she made her living as a physical therapist for more than 30 years.

Then, said Marion, her life hit an iceberg:

When I reached about age 55, people were not very interested anymore in physical therapy. And the doctors who had been sending people to me began retiring or died. And so I thought I would just wait it out until I got Social Security and sit down and wait until I died. That's what I thought would happen.

Hardly. During her gloomy transition, Marion rediscovered a fascination with the body-mind connection that, over time, she developed into a pioneering approach to therapeutic bodywork. Now, more than four decades later, the highly successful Rosen Method continues to be taught and offered by a professional network of more than 2,000 practitioners at locations in the United States and 14 other countries.

Just Do It

Reinventing ourselves on such a scale seems unique only because so few of us ever envision or attempt it, says pioneering researcher Michael Murphy, whose work in the field of human potential has filled thousands of pages and spanned nearly six decades.

Shortly after his own seventy-eighth birthday, Mike told me this:

> To the extent that you can find your bliss when you're young, God bless. But at least, when you've got another 10, 20, 30 years left, jump in there!
>
> In the second half of life, you and I have stored up stuff that can be harvested. We're ripe for it. All this surplus energy is there. There is this stupendous creative opportunity.
>
> Yes, it's hard. Joseph Campbell and following your bliss— that doesn't mean sitting around floating in the Bahamas. Sometimes there's a lot of suffering in pushing your way through.
>
> The secret is in knowing that it's better to fail at your own bliss than succeed at someone else's. Realizing your human potential means using the life you are given to become more and more of who you really are. It means: Just do it!

Because our fascination provides us an initial sense of direction, discovering and deciphering it is the imperative first step in the design of our reinvention.

But it's when we begin to move forward in the direction found—*to translate our inner pushes and pulls into real-world action and goals*—that we truly know we're on the right path.

For, if we have indeed discovered our bliss, our fascination, then the "just doing of it" will inevitably produce an unparalleled level of energy and joy.

This is the elixir of the reinvention process, the mysterious element that propels success—and successful people—of all kinds.

It is the stuff called *flow*.

Step 2. Find Your Flow
(Ask: What Kind of Work Will Turn My Fascination into Flow?)

Real-Time Reinvention

I still remember my "eureka" moment and the thought that accompanied it: "So that's what this is all about!"

I had experienced it while running and playing competitive tennis, but it happened more frequently—and markedly—in my early thirties, when I began doing live TV news.

In the start-up days at CNN, the Washington news bureau was quite small. My assignments included live reports from the White House or the Capitol as many as 10 times a day. In the early morning hours or evening, I anchored hourlong live programs that included interviews on controversial issues with high-ranking government officials.

Whether in the field or at the anchor desk, the experience was the same: I had the strangest feeling that I wasn't really there!

In between broadcasts, I was continually absorbing information—in briefings, on the phone, from the newswires. I had constant deadlines, an empty stomach, and a chronic caffeine headache. On the biggest news days, like the day President Reagan was nearly assassinated, the pressure was extraordinary.

There was no room for error and even less time to prepare.

More often than I should admit, I stepped in front of a live national audience with no script and no clear plan for what I was about to say.

Yet it was in these situations that my best work frequently occurred.

My brain was somehow able to access and organize details I had not consciously memorized. Words that were not part of my everyday vocabulary just came rolling out.

During these experiences, I often felt like I was "flying" out of control.

But later I could see, in reviewing the videotapes, that I had appeared confident and comfortable, no matter what was going on. It looked as though a much more seasoned news correspondent was channeling through me, and I was becoming him.

I was being reinvented in real time.

While these experiences were occurring, they were often scary, even painful. But when they were over, they felt like the most fun I'd ever had.

I asked close friends about them—a professional football player, a software engineer, a stockbroker, an orthopedic resident. Each reported episodes like mine, when tackling work that they loved.

But what was happening remained a mystery to me until a professor at the University of Chicago with a long, strange name wrote a book that nailed it. He called this phenomenon *flow*, the optimal human experience.

That's what this was all about!

The Father of Flow

Mihaly Csikszentmihalyi (pronounced "cheeks-sent-me-high") was barely a teenager when the Communist Party completed its political, social, and economic takeover of Hungary following World War II.

One of his brothers was killed in combat; another was taken prisoner by the Russians and sent to a Siberian labor camp. His father, Alfred, was fired from his post as Hungary's ambassador to Italy, and wound up running a restaurant in Rome.

Back home in Budapest, numerous relatives and close family friends—previously members of the Hungarian upper crust— had been killed. The lives of those who survived were forever altered: their social standing and financial security evaporated.

In the midst of this chaos, young Csikszentmihalyi grew obsessed with a question: Why was it that although most people seemed emotionally devastated by the losses they had suffered, a very few remained serene and in control?

"As a child in the war, I'd seen something drastically wrong with how adults—the grown-ups I trusted—organized their thinking," explained Csikszentmihalyi. "I was trying to find a better system to order my life."[12]

In his early twenties, the search for such a system led him to emigrate to the United States, where he earned a doctorate at the University of Chicago and was eventually named a full professor of human development.

Chicago gave him the freedom to pursue massive, multiyear studies into the nature of human experience, work that generated volumes of real-life data and gave birth to the concept of flow.

It was a breakthrough that turned the fields of psychology and peak performance inside out.

The Flow of Self-Chosen Goals

Csikszentmihalyi had investigated all the popular approaches to optimum living, and was unimpressed. Having personally seen some of the worst things that life can offer, he considered most so-called keys to happiness pure theory, and superficial at that.

His studies—first begun in the 1970s—broke the mold. His objective was first to gain access to the reality—what he termed the *phenomenology*—of our inner experience, then to calculate how best to manage it for maximum results.

Wrote Csikszentmihalyi: "My work consisted of developing a systematic phenomenology to answer the question: What is life like? And the more practical question: How can each person create an excellent life?"[13]

This inquiry would require a scientific approach, so Csikszentmihalyi and his colleagues invented one.

Bypassing traditional techniques like polls, surveys, and diaries, they developed a "live" feedback system called the *experience sampling method* (ESM) whereby pagers or programmable watches were planted on individuals for weeks, sometimes months at a time.

The idea was to create a "virtual filmstrip" of people's daily activities and how they experienced them "inside."

When participants were signaled at random times, their instructions were to jot down answers to questions like: Where are you? What are you thinking about? Who are you with? What are you doing—working, relaxing, studying, eating, doing chores, driving, or something else?

Most significantly, they were asked to make a note of their subjective experiences: How are you feeling? How happy are you? How motivated are you? Would you rather be doing something else?

Data was collected over years from thousands of people—ranging from teenagers to the elderly—in every walk of life. All of it, concluded Csikszentmihalyi, pointed to one unmistakable bottom line:

> *Contrary to what we usually believe, . . . the best moments in our lives are not the passive, receptive, relaxing times. The best moments usually occur when a person's body or mind is stretched to its limit in a voluntary effort to accomplish something difficult or worthwhile. Optimal experience is thus something we make happen.*[14]

Because so many of the people he studied reported feeling as though they were flying or "floating" during these moments of voluntary accomplishment, Csikszentmihalyi labeled what they were experiencing *flow*, which he defined as the highest level of human happiness.

In doing so, he codified that which he'd been seeking since childhood—a system for excellent living based not on theory but on empirical evidence from real life.

Flow is generated when fascination is translated into action. Flow, the highest level of human happiness, is the source of peak performance and success.

As they gained attention, Csikszentmihalyi's findings struck a chord with high-performance people in many fields: U.S. President Bill Clinton, British Prime Minister Tony Blair, and leading management experts heralded their implications for productivity and business. Dallas Cowboys coach Jimmy Johnson reportedly used Csikszentmihalyi's first popular book, entitled *Flow*, in preparing for the 1993 Super Bowl.[15]

Yet while Csikszentmihalyi's research was strikingly new, it was grounded in ancient wisdom that dates, at minimum, to the Greeks of Athens, the cradle of western civilization. For what has come to be known as *flow*, Aristotle knew as *eudemonia*—the "'highest good spirit'" as he characterized it: *a state of being that is solely produced*, he wrote, *by virtuous activity of the soul.*

No doubt, this helps explain why many intelligent, successful people throughout the ages made it a point to never stop working. Instead, they set out to *discover and translate their fascination into flow*, and in doing this, they found the secret of long-term success.

Pursuing a Lifetime of Flow

The grandson of Sicilian immigrants, Jack Valenti gave his first political speech—in favor of a local sheriff—from a flatbed truck in Texas, at age 10.

"I never recovered from it," he later wrote.[16]

Valenti never stood taller than 5-foot-7, but throughout his life he always found a way to leverage his fascination with politics and salesmanship into the highest happiness—the flow of accomplishment.

Wherever he went, Valenti was forever campaigning, packaging, promoting his ideas. He came across as charming and harmless, said a reporter, but "he knew how to win."[17]

He talked his way to success.

After piloting B-25s in World War II, Valenti returned to Texas where he helped launch Humble Oil Company's most successful advertising campaign. Then, founding his own Houston ad agency, he won over Conoco, a rival oil company, as one of his biggest clients.

In 1963, Valenti was recruited by Lyndon Johnson to be his top White House advisor. Valenti supervised presidential appearances and speechmaking, and he played a crucial role in the passage of LBJ's Great Society legislation.

From there, he moved on to become president of the Motion Picture Association of America. It was Valenti who personally invented and persuaded Hollywood moguls and movie audiences to adopt the voluntary (G, PG, R, X) rating system that remains in effect today.

For 38 years he was the public face of the U.S. film and TV production industry, and its chief spokesman around the world. He hobnobbed with the likes of Frank Sinatra, Kirk Douglas, and Sophia Loren, and enjoyed regular appearances as a presenter on the Academy Awards.

Four days before his eighty-third birthday, he turned over the top job to a younger man. But he "continued to come to work, nattily dressed" as always, wrote the *New York Times*, and he never ceased generating new ideas and projects.

Among them was his 2007 book entitled *This Time, This Place: My Life in War, the White House and Hollywood* in which he wrote this:

> *Retirement to me is a synonym for decay. The idea of just knocking about, playing golf or whatever, is so unattractive to me that I would rather be nibbled to death by ducks.*
>
> *So long as I am doing what I choose to do and love to do, work is not work, but total fun.*

Valenti passed away a month before he was scheduled to begin a six-city promotional book tour. Heaven only knows what kind of fun he'd have had next.

Through all of his life, he was a work in progress. No matter his age, he never stopped translating his fascination—in his case, with politics, promotion, and salesmanship—into flow, the special joy that comes with tackling self-chosen goals.

In the last part of his career he was fortunate to have a "company job" that allowed him to keep reinventing himself. But no doubt, he would have found a way to do so, regardless.

Psychologists, coaches, and other professionals who have studied flow, call people like Valenti *autotelic*. They work at what they do for the sheer experience—for the sake of the work itself.

Wrote Csikszentmihalyi in *Creativity*, one of his three excellent books on optimal experience: "In one fashion or another, their work—the focused application of all of their skills to a worthy, self-chosen goal—continues until they die or are incapacitated. But, then why call what they are doing work? It may just as easily be called play."[18]

In the process, such people may be, and frequently are, rewarded in other ways—fortune and fame included—but these are not their primary motivations.

Work for them is play, the very doing of it, in Jack Valenti's words, is "total fun."

Translating Your Fascination into Success

I have a friend who's a successful corporate accountant. She has done well enough to own two vacation homes—one in the mountains, and one a few doors down from my full-time home, near the Pacific Coast. Often she'll come down on a beautiful weekend and lock herself inside with a pile of paperwork: "I love to figure things out, to solve problems, to lose track of time," she says.

In a few years, she has told me, she plans to retire. And do what? I've asked. "Oh, not much—what retired people usually do, I guess. Go out to dinner, travel some, and putter around the garden. I'm looking forward to it."

Here, the famous inscription on the entry to Apollo's temple at Delphi begs to be heard: *gnothi seauton*—Know Thyself. Examine your life deeply, and you will come to understand how you really are.

My friend does not know herself nearly well enough.

As an outsider, it's easy for me to see: she doesn't immerse herself in work on the weekends because it's something she needs to do. There's clearly something about it that fascinates her so much that she loses track of time. The reason she loves to figure things out (and based on her track record, you can bet they're complicated) is because this is what makes her happiest.

Complex problems fascinate her. *Solving them is her way of generating flow.*

Recognizing what fascinates and inspires us, what area or direction uniquely "pulls us forward," is the first step in reinventing our success.

Next, we must determine how to translate our fascination into action and flow.

To do so, we must ask ourselves:

What will be my *work* in the area of my fascination?

What kinds of things would I love to do?

How will I choose goals that fit my personality?

What, for me personally, will generate the most flow?

- Jack Valenti loved to make speeches and presentations. This was how he translated his fascination with politics and promotion into "total fun" and lifelong reinvention.

- Dr. Shep Nuland was fascinated by storytelling from the time he was a boy. When he retired after decades as a surgeon, it was in writing medical stories that he generated flow and award-winning success.

- Clinical psychologist Rita Spina, who is among the success stories you will read later, found herself fascinated with environmental issues in her early sixties. For Rita, creating environmentally conscious citizen groups and artwork were the keys to flow and reinvented achievement.

- L.A. District Attorney Gil Garcetti, with whom we will also visit, reinvented himself as a highly paid, world-class photographer by taking pictures of people, places, and things that fascinated him but were barely noticed by anyone else.

While each reinventive individual I've studied, in writing this book, had a unique fascination and chose to pursue distinctly individualized work, all of them experienced uncommon levels of happiness and success.

"When I'm working in my studio, I lose all sense of time," Rita Spina, the psychologist turned community organizer and artist told me. "Anything I may have been worrying about just disappears into the background, and creative ideas appear in their place. It's a wonderful feeling—some of the best moments of my life."

When Shep Nuland was asked by his editor to reread the manuscript of his award-winning book, he said, "I saw things in each paragraph that I couldn't remember having written. I saw a philosophy that I had obviously been living by, but had not been consciously aware of. I was flabbergasted by this! God, . . . did you write this? And then, of course, I thought back, . . . who else could have written this?"

Had he heard these comments, Mihaly Csikszentmihalyi would not, in the least, have been surprised.

While extraordinary, such experiences are not unusual when we tackle self-chosen goals and activities that stretch our abilities and turn our work into a "game of flow."

As mentioned earlier, my introduction to flow's impact came under the pressures of doing live TV news on CNN, a job that I adored. I found myself performing well beyond what I thought my capabilities were, and I felt almost euphoric during and after being on-air. But until I learned what was happening, I didn't recognize flow for what it was.

That's been the case for a lot of people I've known, as it may be for you.

Take a moment to think back on your own times of intense challenge and achievement—perhaps in school, on the playing field, on the stage, or while working.

Which of the following flow "symptoms" have you experienced? What were you doing when this occurred?

Symptoms of the Flow Experience

- **Total immersion:** We're "in the zone." Our goals are clear. Our actions and awareness are merged. We may feel like we're floating or flying, in and out of control.

- **Disappearance of self-consciousness:** We're stretched to the limit but have a sense of strength and confidence in ourselves and our abilities. At times, we may feel like we're not really there.

- **No worries:** Everyday concerns don't clog our attention. Issues like money, health, and relationship problems are out of range. We are free to do and think what, how, and when we want.

- **Distorted sense of time:** Time may slow, accelerate, or seem completely absent. There is no past or future. We live in one extended moment.

- **Sense of joyful mastery:** Sometimes during, but usually following the flow experience, we feel a rush of well-being and a sense of joy, gratitude, and satisfaction. Our muscles may still ache and brains feel like they're scrambled, but we have a distinct sense that, somehow, we have grown.

- **Peak performance:** Unexpected results are produced. Our thinking is clearer, creativity is enhanced, memory is sharper, and speed and timing are improved. Our moves are smarter, scores are higher, and overall results are better than ever.[19]

The last symptom, of course, is considerably more than an internal state. It is a measurable, external reality that can be directly attributed to flow.

Flow Triggers Peak Performance

According to the now-extensive research on the topic, peak performance, and in tandem with it, the expansion of our abilities and success, are regular and quantifiable consequences of the flow experience.

This is why the study of flow—how best to trigger and manage it—has, in recent years, become a crucial element in the training of professional athletes, dancers, software engineers, and top performers in a wide range of fields.

In training of this nature, participants are coached to fall in love with the game itself, rather than concentrate on the outcome.

Csikszentmihalyi writes: "When we act freely, for the sake of action rather than ulterior motives, . . . and invest ourselves in it to the limits of our concentration, whatever we do will be enjoyable. And once we have tasted this joy, we will redouble our efforts to taste it again. After each episode of flow a person becomes a unique individual, possessed of rarer skills. This is how the self grows."[20]

Put another way: *translating our personal fascination into flow leads not only to the highest level of human happiness but, predictably, to peak performance, growth, and success.*

On paper, the process looks something like this:

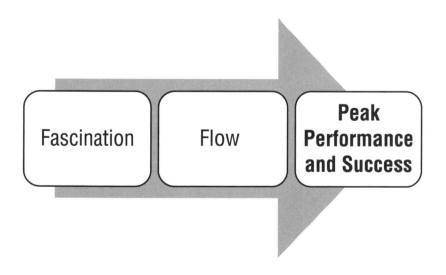

The Bottom Line

How will my friend, the corporate accountant who loves solving problems, design the rest of her life?

Will she retire to her garden in search of happiness? Or will she come to better understand herself? To translate her fascination into a new kind of work she can love—and succeed at—for the long term?

What will you and I do?

If successful reinvention is our choice, we must take these steps:

Three Steps to Successful Reinvention

Step 1. Discover your fascination.
Ask: What is the direction that pulls me forward?
Step 2. Find your flow.
Ask: What kind of work will turn my fascination into flow?
Step 3. Envision your structure.
Ask: Will I create a project, a role, a career, a business, or a nonprofit?

Structuring our reinventive work is the topic of the next chapter.

chapter four

Structuring
Your Future

Success Story: Horace Deets

*Get up right now and go to the window. Open it, and
stick your head out and yell, . . . I'm mad as hell and
I'm not going to take this anymore.*
—Patty Chayefsky, *Network*

A s I traveled coast-to-coast to visit with successfully reinventive men and women—no matter where or how they had grown up, the kinds of careers they had built in the first half of life, or the nature of the work they had developed since— one salient characteristic stood out: *an entrepreneurial spirit.*

They felt it was preposterous that the conventional map of life calls for intelligent, accomplished people to begin readying themselves for obsolescence shortly after midlife. They thought it absurd that so many people unquestioningly went along with this.

And they were willing to *invent* whatever avenues or opportunities they found necessary to pursue their fascinations, generate flow, and unlock their full potential.

Nowhere was this attitude more striking—startling might better describe it—than in the case of Horace B. Deets.

After decades building a distinguished career in what many call "the most important city in the world," Horace was dubbed "Washington D.C.'s Second Most Powerful Man" by *Fortune* magazine. Four years later, at age 63, when many of his counterparts were activating retirement plans, Horace chose to buck conventional thinking and seek fresh territory for achievement.

"Before," he told me, "I could fly Business Class and give a talk at the European Union headquarters. Now, people don't return my calls or answer my letters. But I expected it."

In fact, for Horace, sacrificing the perks of power was just part of the plan:

> *I knew a lot of former senators, members of Congress, and generals who told me that the shelf life of a former anything in Washington is about one nanosecond. So it simply indicated a transition from one phase of my life to the next.*
>
> *I think the common mindset is you stop working and you play golf or you go fishing for a few years and then you die. Not me. The question I have is: Where are the things that I can have the biggest impact on, that will be the most meaningful?*
>
> *By God, people say, at 66 or 67, there's not much you can do. But for me, that's just plain crazy. It's the rest of my life, for God's sake!*

I included part of this quotation in Chapter 1 of this book, but I intentionally did not mention its source. I was saving that, and the exquisite irony behind Horace's story, until now.

You see, the organization Horace built into the most influential advocacy force in the United States is AARP, the American Association of *Retired* People.

As AARP's executive director, he grew its membership to more than 33 million men and women, nearly 1 in every 5 registered voters.

But long before walking away from this political powerhouse he constructed, he made a decision *not to retire*—not then, or ever, if he could help it.

It was a resolution rooted deeply in his psyche:

My dad used to say, when I first went to work for AARP, "Don't send me a membership card." And I would say, "Why's that?" He would say, "Because I'm not ready to retire." I would say, "Why's that, Dad? You're eligible to." And he would say, "Well, I've noticed that a lot of my friends have retired, and a year later I'm going to their funerals. And I don't give a damn what the coroner thinks, I think they died of boredom. And that's not going to happen to me!"

So I had a model in my father, but I also had other models, people I met along the way. I made the decision for myself early. I did a traditional retirement from AARP, but that didn't mean I was retiring from life—or from work.

Although he was approached with a number of post-AARP job offers, he had something in mind other than short-term "retirement work."

Horace's objective was reinventing himself for *long-term success*.

And, given his background in workforce management, he was keenly aware of several things. First, the workplace is not accustomed to 60-plus-year-olds with aspirations like his. Second, like others whose ambitions have collided with the traditional map of life, whatever opportunities or structures he needed to accomplish his goals, he would likely have to create on his own.

And so he did:

I'm not an artist. I'm not a musician. That's not my form of creativity. I guess what I've created is a role that I'm happy with — I'm something like a freelance do-gooder. My fascination is to be part of something that can truly make a difference in people's lives. I really want to pick and choose, to do things that I find important and relevant. The things that I have done, that I can do, I want to perpetuate. I want to build and grow and expand and diversify them.

Upon leaving AARP, he forged strategic arrangements to serve as a board member and advisor to organizations with which he had previous connections and shared a common goal: addressing the challenges of older people around the world. Among them were nonprofits such as Help Age International, MIT's Age Lab, and Oxford University's Center on Aging, as well as profit-driven firms including the Longevity Alliance and Posit Science Incorporated.

Horace structured win-win alliances with these groups: they could leverage his incomparable knowledge of the aging field, including its complex politics and demographics.

In turn, Horace could work at his fascination — a love for coaching, mentoring, and developing people that dated back to his twenties, when he was ordained a Catholic priest and assigned to be a high school teacher and administrator in Charleston, South Carolina:

What I like to do is coach, mentor, train, and watch people grow. That's what excites me. As a teacher, I loved watching when someone had the "a-ha" or eureka moment. Particularly when you'd watch them wrestle with something, and you'd see their head and eyes come up—I've got it! Right on! That, for me, makes the day worthwhile.

As things evolved, Horace's transition, from Washington power broker to agent of empowerment, proved to be financially rewarding, as well:

Whereas I worked for nonprofits all my life, now I'm working with two boards of profit-making companies. And to be frank, it's a somewhat novel experience for me. I think a lot of my colleagues who are former priests, like I am, find the same thing. But with the organizations I'm working with, I want them to be successful because their missions matter to me personally.

When I first met Horace at the Aspen Institute seminar on life's second half, mentioned earlier in the book, he immediately stood out. There, among people considerably younger, was this then 67-year-old who, for decades, had famously represented the interests of millions of traditional retirees but who never for a moment had subscribed to their thinking or lifestyle.

As I got to know him better, I never ceased to be inspired by his personal reinvention or struck by his stalwart repudiation of the conventional life structure that had been passed down by previous generations.

Horace considered it an invisible virus—unhealthy to body, mind, and society and insidiously resistant to change:

> We've all been infected by it. Many of us had our mindsets locked in by age five. What we were taught way-back-when about getting older has never been retooled and updated. We act the way we think we're supposed to act at certain ages. We divide life into: you learn, you work, you do leisure. No overlap, please. Well, that's crap!

Horace's bluntness may be singular, but among those who have thought deeply on these issues, he is not alone in his appraisal or sense of indignation.

Phyllis Moen, chair of sociology at the University of Minnesota, has spoken and written scathingly about what she calls the "lockstep" of our lives. Says Moen, we have bought into a "package of institutionalized age-based expectations" that "starts with full-time education in youth, moves to a lifetime of continuous, full-time employment, and culminates in a one-way, one-time, irreversible exit into a full-time leisure called 'retirement.' This, we are told, is the path to the American dream."[1]

Writer William Sadler has called this our "unconscious map of life," so outdated and ineffective as to be "like world maps used before Columbus sailed."

An Entrepreneurial Mindset

However we characterize it—lockstep, package, stereotype, or myth—this model is the way life has been structured in America, and elsewhere, for most of the past century. And however anachronistic, its chokehold on societal thinking remains exceedingly tight.

It is precisely for this reason that there is no established career track today for people who are beyond midlife. And it is why those of us who aspire to discover our full lifetime potential will need to *step out of line*, to follow the examples of Horace Deets, Shep Nuland, and the other reinventive people you will meet in this book.

Once these men and women determined what type of work would fascinate them and bring them flow, they tackled the third step in the *Design of Reinvention*—they set out to envision and create marketplace structures and opportunities that would allow them to pursue their new work and achieve their long-term personal goals.

Each took on the responsibility that management expert Peter Drucker recommended for all of us in the new knowledge economy: they became chief executive officers of themselves.

They made the transition to personal entrepreneurship.

Step 3. Envision Your Structure (Ask: Will I Create a Project, a Role, a Career, a Business, or a Nonprofit?)

As we continue to examine successfully reinvented men and women, we will explore the creative ways they addressed this challenge, the unique practices they developed, and the uncommon joy of their results.

Later we will travel, as well, into the little-known realm of advanced intelligence and creativity to see how unexpected talents, wisdom, and luck often emerge to further our goals in midlife and beyond.

But what's most important to appreciate at this point is that *reinvention begins with an entrepreneurial heart and mindset.*

Here, I am using the term *entrepreneurial* not only in the sense of independently creating a livelihood, vocational niche, or business structure but in the broader spirit of the original French verb *entreprendre*, which means "to undertake" one's own future, to own and manage all of its opportunities, risks, and rewards.

Why, you might ask, is this necessary? Why not just search for the *perfect new employer or job?*

Because, as we are about to see, the age-related stereotypes that have long shaped society's thinking have permeated the workplace in spades.

This is a fact of life that, for all too many of us, may come as a rude surprise.

▶ **CLAIM:** Corporate America has plenty of jobs for experienced knowledge workers.

✔ **REALITY CHECK:** As we move through life's second half, private sector companies are not likely venues for personal reinvention.

Beginning in the early 2000s, survey after survey of career men and women in midlife and beyond reported that a significant transformation was underway: an unprecedented and growing percentage of people needed, wanted, and were "expecting to continue working at the point where earlier generations moved to the sidelines" and into retirement.[2]

Rather than "freedom from work," surveys indicated, many were excited about retiring from their current positions and having the freedom to *work at new jobs* that would provide them with continuing income, purpose, and professional relationships well into their seventies or longer.

Their optimism was contagious and widespread:

"Employers will be lucky to have me."

"At this age, my experience speaks for itself."

"I'll just use a recruiter and find something great."

What's more, a number of career-oriented websites and at least one nationally known career consultancy publicized the notion that "older workers will be in great demand" in the twenty-first century. The evidence pointed to was a "projected shortage" of millions of intelligent, skilled workers, with experienced older people "primed to fill such spots."[3]

Deeper research, however, suggests a very different workplace reality: *if you're an intelligent, successful person in midlife or beyond, the best job you may ever have going forward may be the role that you personally create.*

Wall Street Journal: "The Retirement Lies We Tell Ourselves"

Not retaining or accommodating: The *Wall Street Journal* has reported that many workers in their fifties and sixties have "a tough time keeping the jobs they have—never mind finding new jobs in retirement." Citing a study by the management consulting firm McKinsey & Company, the paper reported that 40 percent of retirees surveyed had been forced to stop working earlier than planned, "a consequence primarily of layoffs or poor health."[4] In separate studies involving 1,400 U.S. organizations, Boston College concluded that employers were "lukewarm" about keeping older workers, and Manpower, Inc. found that less than 30 percent of companies had a formal strategy to retain them, while only 18 percent had a program to recruit them.[5]

New York Times: "Happy Birthday. Vacate Your Office."

Still offloading: While mandatory retirement at a certain age is now outlawed in most cases, de facto retirement policies remain in place. Experienced corporate executives and well-paid professionals—physicians, attorneys, and journalists among them—often feel intense pressure to "make room for new blood." Additionally, employers historically have not been reluctant to utilize economic dips, mergers, or corporate restructurings as rich opportunities to offload workers with the most seniority. And despite new laws on the books, in cases of both firing and hiring, age discrimination remains extremely difficult to prove in court.[6]

New York Times: "For a Good Retirement, Find Work, Good Luck."

Not really hiring: If older workers do lose their jobs, according to Alicia Munnell, director of the Center for Retirement Research at Boston College, "then it's horrible. They have a much harder time finding work again than younger job seekers." Despite the superior experience and judgment they might bring to the table, companies remain "leery of hiring" older workers due to concerns that they are less energetic, productive, and adaptable and more likely to have outdated skills, Texas A&M economist Joanna Lahey told the *New York Times*. "The effects of such discrimination are personal injustice and economic inefficiency." She added, "The labor market for older workers is broken."[7]

This bottom line was the expert consensus in the summer of 2008, during the relatively early stages of the Great Recession, the deepest economic downturn since the 1930s.

A little more than a year later, the Mature Market Institute, the recognized leader on longevity and workplace issues, completed a major national study on the "new realities of the job market" for people in midlife and beyond.[8]

It was entitled, quite starkly: "Buddy, Can You Spare a Job?" Based on labor analysis, workplace data, and authoritative interviews, researchers laid out the facts: the unemployment rate for post-midlife workers had more than doubled from 2007 to 2009, to the highest level in at least 60 years. Hence, "there will be millions of baby boomers looking for work to prolong their careers in the years ahead."

There's just one problem, workforce specialists underscored: *the job market has other plans.*

"The expectations older boomers have about working after 55 are often painfully unrealistic," according to their report.

First, age bias is both a serious obstacle to their staying employed as well as a major barrier to their obtaining new employment, a situation for which "earnest, well-prepared job seekers in their fifties and sixties are often totally unprepared."

Second, given the immense metrics involved, "there is a compelling disconnect between the growing size and availability" of the pool of mature job candidates and the number of opportunities that are, or may become, available to them.

In a separate report issued a year later, entitled "The New Unemployables," public policy experts at Rutgers University concluded: "We are witnessing the birth of a new class—the involuntarily retired."[9]

▶ **CLAIM:** Nonprofit and volunteer organizations will provide opportunities for personal reinvention.

✔ **REALITY CHECK:** Maybe, but it's hard to tell.

A number of experts are hopeful that the nonprofit workplace—organizations that provide health care, education, government, and social services—will, over time, provide fresh openings for experienced people, where the private sector does not.

Some point to research conducted in 2008 by Peter D. Hart Research Associates, a premier national polling firm, indicating that some 5 million Americans, between the ages of 44 and 70, had managed, over the preceding decade or so, to land full- or part-time salaried positions in the nonprofit sector "serving the greater good," after leaving their primary careers.[10]

Further, an additional 40 million were said to be interested in doing the same—in finding what some call *encore careers*.

But realistically, going forward, how many will pull this off?

The same researchers also surveyed 427 nonprofit employers and found this: while most nonprofits said they found the idea of bringing in late career or previously retired workers appealing, *in the majority of organizations, more than three-quarters of current employees were under the age of 50.*[11]

Moreover, in their most recent employment decisions, nonprofits that hired applicants who were just starting out in their careers outnumbered those hiring late career workers by more than a third.

One school of economists predicts change: they project an expansion, even a labor shortage in some nonprofit fields, in the decades ahead.[12]

But will nonprofit hiring priorities shift as well? Will more experienced workers get the nod? And, if so, would they truly be able to reinvent themselves—to carve out work that fascinates and develops them—or might they wind up in lower-paying, dead-end jobs?

If the past is in any way predictive, it's hard to say.

Will You Do Laundry?

Consider this story, from *Fortune* magazine, headlined: "Candy Striper, My Ass!"

▶ AFTER 33 YEARS AT KODAK, where he had become president of the company's Mexico operations, Don Spieler, 64, decided to retire and volunteer his time, knowledge, and business acumen in his hometown of Rochester, New York.

Like many other successful individuals, he felt that he'd been fortunate during his career and wanted to give something—more than just a financial contribution—back to the community.

Upon arriving home in Rochester, he stopped in at the United Way, where he envisioned himself sitting on the board of directors or managing grantees. The local United Way director seemed thrilled to meet him, but a few weeks later a staffer called with his assignment: fund-raising.

Spieler had never volunteered to raise money, and it

wasn't how he wanted to spend his time: "I was pissed off," he said.

"Over the next two years," the *Fortune* article continued, "Spieler went to seven different nonprofit organizations; at nearly all, he was asked to do work that was boring or that ignored his expertise."

One asked him to volunteer as an office manager for two days a week. The Chamber of Commerce wanted him to attend meetings and write up the minutes. Concluded Spieler: "I found an entrenched group of agencies that did not accept the skills I could provide for them."[13]

Perhaps you've had a personal experience like his? Working on this book, I met more than a few people who have.

One woman I spoke with, a high-powered private college administrator, told me she couldn't count the number of times she'd tried to "give back" to an educational nonprofit, only to end up "sucked into busy work on some kind of committee."

What goes on here?

Take this incident, from the *Chronicle of Higher Education*:

▶ "AFTER A DISTINGUISHED MEDICAL CAREER spanning four decades," Dr. Dorothea Glass, a professor and president of a major physician's association in Philadelphia, retired to Palm Beach County in Florida. "After a few months of R&R, she was climbing the walls with boredom," and she approached a local hospital.

"Put me to work in a way that makes use of my experience and my passion for medicine," she volunteered, "and you can have my services free of charge."

"After some consideration," reported the *Chronicle*, "the hospital informed Dr. Glass that they were pleased to offer her a new volunteer position—refilling water pitchers."[14]

I'll Just Do It Myself

Certainly, incidents like these don't tell the entire story.

There unquestionably are, and will be, nonprofits willing to employ the skills and contributions of men and women who want to make a difference in life's second half.

But as the demographic waves of such people grow, some nonprofit insiders warn of a "big bang," a grand mismatch between well-intentioned individuals and the status quo.

"To be frank, most nonprofits aren't ready to make the most of their experience," writes Robert Egger, CEO of D.C. Central Kitchen and author of *Begging for Change: The Dollars and Sense of Making Nonprofits Responsive, Efficient, and Rewarding for All.*[15]

"Will former heads of corporate human resource departments be satisfied painting walls or sorting food donations?" he asks. "We cannot make the mistake of trying to fit this round generation's promise into a square volunteer box." Egger has urged the nonprofit sector to "get ready—there's no time to waste."

Some people, however, got tired of waiting a long time ago.

A growing number of mature men and women have become self-inspired *social entrepreneurs*, taking the needs of communities, the nation, and the world into their own hands: structuring their own opportunities, roles, organizations, and solutions to educational, environmental, health, and other societal challenges.

A significant percentage of the nonprofits established each year in the United States are mom-and-pop start-ups. Many are created when men and women in midlife and beyond put their unique personal fascinations to work on problems that others are unaware of or choose to ignore.

Not all social entrepreneurships succeed, of course, but some develop award-winning track records. Each of the following, for instance, was started by people over age 60:

Third World Development

The *Full Belly Project* was started by Jock Brandis, a former movie lighting director in Wilmington, North Carolina. He took on the mission of inventing and distributing income-generating agricultural devices to improve life in rural Africa.

Environment

The *Green Science Policy Institute* was the brainchild of chemist Arlene Blum in Berkeley, California. She was fascinated with the idea of limiting household toxins by creating working collaborations between scientists, industry, and consumers.[16]

Community Health and Nutrition

The *Prime Time Sister Circles* was a project brought into existence by two Washington, D.C., health professionals: physician Marilyn Gaston and clinical psychologist Gayle Porter. The goal was to empower African American women to improve their health through peer support and existing social networks in sororities, churches, and community organizations.

Upon being honored at Stanford University for her project's achievements, Dr. Gaston, a former assistant U.S. surgeon general, underscored the challenges faced by even the most ambitious of us who would seek to extend our records of accomplishment into life's second half.

"We have all this experience that nobody appreciates and wants to mine," said Gaston. "We're people just ready-made to be tapped."[17]

Trailblazing the Future

Accomplished men and women may be ready to reinvent their success records, but there are limited ready-made opportunities to do so in twenty-first-century America.

By the time we reach our fifties, the private sector is reluctant to take us on. Future opportunities may develop in the non-profit sector, but it's difficult to tell.

How, then, do you and I move forward in midlife and beyond?

The solution, once again, is clear:

> **If we cannot reinvent ourselves within existing structures, we will need to invent our own.**

Certainly, it's reasonable to ask: How did things come to be this way?

Why is there no significant national infrastructure dedicated to tapping our resources? To capitalizing on the tens of millions of us who are expected to live longer, healthier lives than any society in human history?

Well, actually, there is—in a manner of speaking.

That's the subject of the next chapter.

Diverted to the Desert

How America Got Hooked on Retirement

I will bring you up out of affliction . . . unto a land of
milk and honey.
— Exodus 3:17

Ninety minutes northwest of Disney World, in what was once Florida pastureland, sits an amusement park of a different kind.

"It resembles a set from *Leave It to Beaver*," observed writer Andrew Blechman, who gave it a look-see from the inside: "Wally and the Beaver are nowhere to be seen. There are no bicycles or baseball mitts littering the yards; no school buses. For that matter there are no children. There aren't even any young couples holding hands. Lawn sprinklers effortlessly turn on and then off in near unison. The lawns are perfectly edged, and try as I might, I can't find a single weed."[1]

Welcome to The Villages, the largest legally age-segregated—sorry—"active retirement" community in the world.

Stretching across the borders of three Florida counties and two zip-codes, The Villages boasts everything its developers envisioned that America's 55-plus-year-olds would and would not want. To start, no one under the age of 19 is allowed as a permanent resident on the 33 square miles (an area larger than Manhattan) that The Villages' daily newspaper, radio, and cable TV stations and billboards call "Florida's friendliest hometown."

For those who are qualified to live among the more than 75,000 residents, The Villages, according to its promoters, is a place where "dreams can come true," from the break of day until late at night. And they have plenty of evidence to back them up.

Locals can ride one of 38,000 golf carts over 100 miles of trails to play 216 privately owned par 3 to 5 holes—at no extra charge—for the rest of their lives.

"The only thing I worry about these days is my golf game," said one retiree.[2]

But there's much more to be concerned with around these parts.

Between visits to the 2 malls, 9 shopping centers, and 60 restaurants on the property, you can "be busy as bees," at dozens of adjacent recreation centers, according to the *Recreation News* activity column. In any given week, more than 70 separate bridge playing and mah-jongg events are on the schedule, not to mention meetings of the following clubs: acoustic guitar, air gun, allamanda pitch league, aloha hula dance, aquatic dancers, archery, aviation, backgammon, badminton, ballet, band, basket weaving, basketball for men, basketball for women, baton twirling, baton with drums and flags, beading, bike riding, and bunco. Of the 1,400 standard happenings at The Villages, these are but a few at the top of the alphabetical menu (I'm not making this up—check www.thevillages.com).

And once the day is under way, things can truly heat up.

At "Katie Belle's" residents-only saloon, regulars gather early for live music and "a great time," Sundays included.

In his book *Leisureville: Adventures in America's Retirement Utopias*, Andrew Blechman writes of his drop-in visit: "An enormous Tiffany-style skylight catches my eye, as do two dozen line dancers keeping time with a country and western tune. Most of the stools along the bar are filled with retirees holding draft beers. I look at my watch. It's just past two in the afternoon."[3]

Asked about his favorite activities, a man named Frank, who'd already had two heart attacks and a stroke, told Blechman, "I'm not much of a cook, so I just eat a lot of pepperoni," after which he likes to "get high and play Nintendo."[4]

But others, apparently, prefer to score in a different way.

While more than 80 percent of residents at The Villages are married, in 2006, local and national news media reported several outbreaks of sexually transmitted diseases—most notably herpes and HPV—maladies generally seen in a much younger population.

Gynecologist Collen McQuade was reported to have treated at least one female patient in her eighties and to have seen more cases of STDs at The Villages than she did in her years of medical practice in Miami. Another physician blamed the high incidence of disease on a lack of sex education and the use of Viagra.

"I'm so horny," one woman told an interviewer. "I gotta use it before I lose it!"

"Whatever your retirement dream," reads The Villages' website, "you're sure to find it here."

Is every retirement haven like this? Of course not.

The Villages is the largest of them all; and, undoubtedly, if you design a "village" on this scale, all kinds of "interesting" people and behaviors will show up.

But more to the point: how did *any* community, segregated by age and dedicated solely to the pursuit of "a permanent vacation," come into existence to begin with?

And how did this kind of a place, one "not of creation but of recreation and vegetation" in the words of historian Daniel Boorstin, *become* "the most conspicuous American institution,"[5] the bedrock structure for the second half of life?

The story of G. Stanley Hall of Massachusetts begins to frame the answer.

The More Things Change

The year was 1921—the year the Miss America Pageant was born in Atlantic City, the World Series was first broadcast on radio, and Adolf Hitler launched the Sturmabteilung, the "brown shirt" paramilitary organization that would play a key role in his rise to power.

It was also the year that *Atlantic Monthly* magazine ran an article by prominent psychologist G. Stanley Hall, who had recently left his job as founding president of Clark University in Worcester, Massachusetts.

Wrote the 77-year-old Hall: "After well-nigh half a century of almost unbroken devotion to an exacting vocation, I lately retired, . . . and there seems nothing more to be said of me save the exact date of my death."[6]

Hall lamented that there was no apparent "curriculum for the later years of life" and called for a "new story" atop the structure of human existence.

"Now I am divorced from my world," he continued. "I really want, and ought, to do something useful and with unitary purpose. But what, and how shall I find it?"

Sound familiar? Wrapped in the vernacular of the 1920s, it is precisely the question we are considering throughout this book: *What's worth doing with a long, healthy life?*

On stepping down from his leadership post at Clark, Hall had found himself on the cusp of a new old age. He had time to spend but no place to go, a role without a reason. He had been thrust into a new "unstable space," according to cultural historian Thomas R. Cole, just beginning to open up in the American lifespan.[7]

Prior to the early twentieth century, except for the very wealthy, free time was largely a pipe dream. You were born, you worked and/or raised a family, and then you died. Some people lived a few extra years of dependence upon their children near the end of life. There was no such thing as "retirement."[8]

Yet, what did not exist would eventually become an immense national problem.

At about the same time that modern health care began to add decades to workers' lives, the Great Depression kicked them off the assembly line. When the economy eventually recovered, it was mostly younger workers who were hired or hired back.

Thereafter, big business turned that which had been born of bad times into what it considered good dollars and sense. Not only on the factory floor but going forward into the information age, the private sector asked: *Why employ older workers when you can hire younger ones for less? Why not download people with seniority as early as you can?*

Out of this thinking emerged the institution of workplace seniority and, along with it, the development of "mandatory" retirement deadlines.

As a result, the "unstable space" that G. Stanley Hall had fallen into began to widen inside millions of American lives.

"Between the 1920s and the 1960s," according to historian Cole, "the reconstruction" of the American life course "proceeded on the assumption that most (older) people cannot contribute significantly to the real world" and thus should be set aside.

Through the decades to follow, bitter skirmishes between labor, business, and government resulted in transformative fiscal policies that would cement this understanding into a new social contract: corporate pensions were drawn up for the first time, and Social Security was launched to provide a financial safety net for life's new extended second half.

By midcentury, Social Security benefits, which had started out small, were expanded to include farm and domestic workers, and the benefits increased by an average of 77 percent. Annual cost-of-living increases were approved, and, not long after, the law was amended to include health insurance benefits under Medicare. Soon, close to 20 million Americans were covered by private pensions, and a million more were added yearly.[9]

With the fear of poverty and illness beginning to diminish, many workers felt less pushed out of the job market than pulled into a new, attractively subsidized way of life.

And the statistics showed it: at the start of the twentieth century, more than 65 percent of men over age 65 were still in the workforce. By 1970, that rate had nearly been cut in half; by the end of the century, it was down to 17.5 percent.[10] Over the same period, the proportion of women in the workforce tripled, from 19 to 60 percent overall. But by the year 2000, only 10 percent of women over 65 were still on the job.[11]

The notion that people should stop working at a certain point of life had been more than institutionalized—it had been elevated into a cultural phenomenon. Not only had retirement become cool, the idea of *early* retirement began to glitter as well.

From multiple angles it appeared that things were coming up roses in life's second half. But beneath the surface, a still-lingering question was gaining strength.

A Place in the Sun

Had you pulled *Time* magazine off the newsstand on Friday, August 3, 1962, you could have read its lead story, headlined "A Place in the Sun."

The article opened with a profile of a 65-year-old retiree, but "not what anybody would call an old man. Though his hair was grey, his face remained unwrinkled, and his voice and hands were quite strong," the magazine said.[12]

Staring out from the New Jersey porch where he was watching over his granddaughter, he was quoted as saying: "I don't know what to do with myself these days. The company is right about the retirement age, I suppose; it has to make place for younger men. But what happens to us?"

Decades after he had passed away, here was G. Stanley Hall's post–Clark University predicament in replay—like déjà vu, all over again. Only now, according to *Time*, it was spreading, fast becoming a "cry and question, . . . being heard more often and more urgently everywhere—in Southern drawl and Northern twang, in city and suburbs, cold-water flat and executive suite."

But this time, reported the magazine, an answer was on the horizon.

And on the cover of that issue of *Time*, his full-color portrait superimposed on the image of a shuffleboard court, palm branches swaying in the foreground, was the man who had positioned himself to provide it.

Below his visage the caption read simply: "Builder Del Webb." But he was much more than that.

Home Run in the Desert

Delbert E. Webb had a long history of home runs. A semiprofessional baseball player in his teens and twenties, Webb managed to grow a one-man carpentry business into a giant construction company, initially by landing government projects. His early success in building schools and dormitories in Arizona led to huge federal defense contracts, including three major military bases and a Japanese American internment camp that was, during World War II, the third largest city in Arizona.

Like the magnate-on-the-make that he was, Webb had the instincts of a big-time speculator. In 1945, he bought part interest in the New York Yankees, with the idea of using free passes to generate new business and publicity. The wager paid off in ways he could not have imagined.

During the years he was one of the Yankees' principal owners, the team won 15 American League and 10 World Series Championships.

But it was in a sun-scorched cotton field north of Phoenix that Webb rolled the dice that would land him on the cover of *Time* and launch a new chapter in the American dream.

Combining his experience as a builder of city-sized projects and his success as a purveyor of favorite pastimes, he developed a strategy and placed a new bet: Why not build cities *around* leisure and recreation? Purchase cheap land and construct affordable housing directly *next to* golf courses, swimming pools, shuffleboard courts, shopping centers, restaurants, and bars?

Why not target these developments at the growing population that had no better answer for what to do with their time?

Why not rebrand retirement—change its image from years of aimless boredom into a full-time vacation: "the best years of your life"?

It was no sure thing. Against the prevailing advice of psychiatrists and gerontologists, Webb took a $2 million gamble—big money in those days—that 55-plus-year-olds would be willing to pull up stakes and move away from family and friends to the middle of nowhere.

It turned out to be a very smart bet.

"Retirement changed forever one sunny day in 1960," is how Del Webb's promotional materials recount the grand opening, aptly scheduled on New Year's Day. "Some 100,000 smartly attired guests in dress shorts strode along the sidewalks and streets," marveling at Del Webb's vision come true.[13] According to one report, the first two days alone netted $2.5 million in sales of newly purchased homes.

And thus was born Sun City, Arizona, the prototype for The Villages in Florida (the location we visited at the beginning of this chapter), Leisure World, and dozens of other age-segregated oases that soon mushroomed across the United States.

The "pursuit of happiness" had found a new frontier.

Social entrepreneur Marc Freedman, who has researched Webb's company extensively, wrote: "Sun City and its look-alikes became the emblematic institution. From those small blades of putting-green grass and that collection of modest homes, an entire industry would grow around the dream of retirement as leisure—the 'Golden Years,' a phrase coined by Webb and his company."[14]

This concept would soon represent much more than a real estate sales pitch. While nationwide only a small percentage of retirees actually packed their bags for retirement cities, those who lived in them, according to Freedman, "became aspirational models for millions of others who might not move onto the golf course, but began building their lives around leisure nonetheless."[15]

What *Time* magazine's editors—then considered beacons of public thinking—heralded as "a dramatically successful solution" to aging in 1963, was on the way to becoming a core national philosophy; as former AARP chief Horace Deets described it in the previous chapter: "We divide life into: you learn, you work, you do leisure. No overlap, please."

This unconscious map, our lockstep in life, was packaged in the desert in the early 1960s. But, over time, it would be injected into the national cerebrum by enthusiastic commercial interests—the media, real estate, the financial and insurance industries among them—until, ultimately, it became the American mindset, the unquestioned status quo.

Except, that is, for independent *creative* thinkers who did not buy into it for a second. And here's the ultimate irony: the two leading giants of the retirement industry—Del Webb, who literally put the "Golden Years" on the map, and Horace Deets, who grew AARP into a mega-force in American politics—were exactly such mavericks themselves.

Neither ever moved into the house of leisure—they kept reinventing themselves, instead.

Leading Life's Second Half

I never had a chance to meet Del Webb; he passed away before I started working on this book. But according to those who interviewed him, in his post-midlife years, Webb so relished reaping his full potential that he couldn't stand the thought of spending more than a few hours in one of his own Sun Cities.

While continuing to construct retirement communities, he forever pushed his fascination forward, creating a new goal for himself and his company: to develop the largest gaming organization in the world. This, too, was accomplished, and more.

Between his early sixties and his death from cancer, at age 75, Webb built lavish casinos, hotels, resorts, and entertainment complexes faster than anybody could count them.

A partial list of his post-midlife achievements includes Madison Square Garden, the Anaheim Stadium, the Sahara hotel-casinos in Las Vegas and Lake Tahoe, the Beverly Hilton in Los Angeles, Scottsdale's Shadow Mountain Resort, the Pasadena Museum of Art, and Chris-Town in Phoenix, the first enclosed shopping mall in the West.

Similarly, Horace Deets, still engaged in a wide range of business and nonprofit projects when I visited with him just after his seventy-first birthday, looked on each new year as a fresh opening for reinvention.

When we spoke, Horace challenged me with a series of questions:

Do you know what the human life span is?

Well, I do, because I've researched it. I know that the human life span is at least 122 years, 164 days. There was a woman from Arles France, Jeanne Calment, who lived that. She lived independently until she was 100. Her vision was impaired, her hearing was poor, but she still could joke with people who were studying her. Her mind was still working fine.

So for myself, I keep saying, if you die before 122, you're dying prematurely.

The problem is that most people don't understand how much longer they're going to live. At 65 today, on average, you're going to live another 20 years, and if it's a married couple, one of you is going to make 90. And that's only going to go up—it's not going to go down.

What's happened in the past 100 years is we've added 30 years to life expectancy at birth, so we've got this longevity bonus, for which neither society nor we as individuals are prepared.

So, what *should* we—as individuals and a society—do to prepare for this? I countered, and Horace replied:

It seems to me that the idea of creating your own future is what it's all about—channeling a direction into something that's meaningful and rewarding and makes a difference in the lives of other people. That, I think, is the key.

Some of it you might do in the business or nonprofit world, if that's what suits you, and if earning an income is important. There's a lot of variation, but you do what your individuality permits.

You've got years of experience, you've done all this stuff. View that as practice.

I think the thing to ask yourself is: How and where am I going to direct that knowledge, skill, and experience for the next 30 years?

What will you create?

Moving forward into the twenty-first century, he advised, each of us will need to answer this question for ourselves.

PART TWO

The
Science of
Lifelong Success

chapter six

The Magic Touch

Success Story: Marion Rosen

*If you bring forth what is within you,
what you bring forth will save you.*
—The Gospel according to Thomas

T he deep twinkle in her 92-year-old blue eyes was the first
thing I noticed.

Here was the woman who, in her late fifties, had given
birth to an international phenomenon, a pioneering method of
therapeutic bodywork admired by physicians, psychologists, chi-
ropractors, and other health-care professionals worldwide; here
was the expert who had personally touched thousands of patients
and had built a network of practitioners in 15 nations to carry
forward the organization that bears her name.

Here was *the* Marion Rosen, *at work* on yet another weekend between trips and office appointments, in yet *another* meeting room, with yet another group of people who had come to be
trained by her.

After all this success, I asked her: Why bother?

Because people want it. And if people want me and get some-
thing from it, then I don't see why I shouldn't do it. What
would I do if I wouldn't work? Sit and wait until I die?

Sure, sometimes I come to the office, and I feel grouchy,
and I don't like the people to come in. And I say to myself:
Why should I be here? And then I put my hand on somebody,
and the excitement makes the hair stand up on my skin when
I see what happens with the person under my hands.

And then I see them afterward, showing up in a way that
they had not been before—full of joy, ideas, aliveness, let's
say. I'm making a big difference in people's lives—that is al-
ways the thing. And I have so much fun doing it!

My first encounter with Marion was at a Rosen Method
training session that I had arranged to observe on the coast of
central California.

Early on, when an assistant requested volunteers for Marion
to personally "work" on, hands flew up across the room. Among
the workshop attendees were nurses and physical therapists who
had traveled long distances to study Marion's techniques and to
sample their benefits directly, whenever possible.

Two participants were randomly chosen—a woman and a
man sitting several rows apart. Having come as a visitor—to write
about Marion's success in life's second half—I was uncertain
whether it would be appropriate for me to volunteer myself. But
once I made the decision to do so, I was selected as a demonstra-
tion subject as well.

I can't remember much about the next half hour. When the
first volunteer was asked to lie face down on a massage table and
Marion began discussing the contours of his shirtless back, I start-

ed scouting for an escape route from the meeting room: What had I gotten myself into? Should I bail out while I still could?

But when my turn came to stretch out in the spotlight, the experience was among the most astounding I've ever had. Others had written about Marion's "treatments," that her hands felt like silk running across their skin. And it was so: after decades of doing bodywork, her fingerprints had literally worn away.

After a few uneventful moments, Marion's attention was somehow drawn to my right shoulder blade, on which she placed her hand gently, about three inches from the base of my neck.

In a soft voice that carried a slight German accent, she asked me the strangest question: "What happened here?"

At first, my mind went blank: I had no idea what to say. I frequently had pain in that shoulder, especially when I was under stress. Sometimes, I took a Tylenol or two to relieve it. But, beyond that, I hadn't given it much thought, and no particular injury came to mind.

But Marion remained fixated on the spot: "Why is this so tight?" she asked me. "What happened here when you were a little boy?" As she questioned me, I began to feel a warming sensation—like candle wax melting in the area where her hand had come to rest. My shoulder muscle seemed to relax, almost deflate, in a way I had never experienced before.

Simultaneously, images of my elementary school years flashed before my eyes: walking and laughing in the hall with my classmates. I saw the headmaster who used to come up behind us, clamp his strong fingers onto our small shoulders, and maneuver us into the classroom. It occurred often. It always happened suddenly. We were powerless to stop it. It was frightening and sometimes it really hurt!

Lying there on a table surrounded by onlookers, I felt my lungs spontaneously fill with air, and then release it in one big gush, along with an involuntary sigh so audible that it shocked me.

With that, any remaining tension in my shoulder seemed to totally disappear.

"Good," Marion said, "very good."

But what just happened? I asked her. Was that some kind of magic?

Not at all, she replied, "a little bit of art, but mostly science."

But how did you know it started when I was a boy?

"Experience," said Marion, "many years of experience."

A Fascination Appears

Marion Rosen was born in Nuremberg, Germany, in 1914, the third of four children in her family. Shortly after her birth, her father left to fight in World War I. Her mother was soon deeply involved with another man who occupied her time and attention.

Marion later wrote: "I felt that my mother had left me and I was the gypsy child this family found and took in. My older brother and sister tolerated me but did not want to be with me. I felt like an outsider, looking at life from a different vantage point."[1]

It was the first of many times she would feel this way.

As a teenager, Marion dreamt of becoming a professional dancer, but as she rapidly grew to a height of 5 feet 9 inches, she was excluded from dancing classes.

Soon thereafter, with the rise of Hitler and the Nazi Party, she was forbidden to attend movies, go to restaurants, or enroll in university coursework. Gentiles she had been friends with—including a boyfriend—turned their backs on her.

"Since there was no life left," she told me, she decided to apply for a visa for travel to the United States. But in the process of doing so, an unusual break occurred:

> *Before I left Germany, my mother was receiving physical ther-*
> *apy for a broken leg. She suggested that I speak to her thera-*
> *pist, a woman named Lucy Heyer. Usually I did not listen to*
> *what my mother told me, but luckily this time I did.*

Lucy Heyer worked with her husband, Dr. Gustav Heyer, a psychoanalyst and student of the famous Swiss psychiatrist Carl Jung.

In their Munich office, Lucy's role was to "loosen patients up" with massage and breathing exercises prior to their appointments with her husband. The Heyers had found that with this kind of physical preparation, the course of psychotherapy, for most patients, was shorter and more effective.

Marion was Lucy Heyer's apprentice for two seminal years:

> *She trained me in everything she knew. During this time I*
> *became very familiar with the body and how it was put to-*
> *gether. That knowledge complemented what I was seeing with*
> *her husband's psychiatry. I began to see how they worked to-*
> *gether. And I said to myself: this is my work, I will do it for the*
> *rest of my life.*[2]

But life was not ready to cooperate.

On the night of November 9, 1938—the infamous Kristallnacht—Nazi storm troopers shattered the windows of Jewish stores, burned synagogues, and raided Jewish homes throughout

Austria and Germany. Women and children were brutalized; more than 30,000 men were rounded up for the one-way journey to concentration camps.

Hitler's "final solution" was under way.

Marion fled to England, where her brother was a psychiatric resident at the well-respected Tavistock clinic. Her hope in going there was to apply what she had learned while working with the Heyers.

But the British doctors would have none of it—what she knew was German hocus-pocus, they told her.

It wouldn't work, they said, for traditional psychoanalytic methods to be combined with her nontraditional approach without a professional theory and research that could explain the results.

At age 24, technical research was not something Marion could provide.

Curtly dismissed, Marion's fascination was driven underground. And the brutal reality of wartime Europe took its place: survival became the order of the day.

Swimming the Mainstream

From London, she moved to Stockholm, where she trained to be a professional physical therapist, and then on to the United States, where she was licensed by the Mayo Clinic and began to earn her living in what was then a burgeoning medical specialty.

During the war, physical therapy was much in demand for injured factory workers. Once the fighting ended, the need grew even greater, as wounded soldiers returned home.

Marion settled in northern California, where, over a career of 35 years, she worked with injured patients at Kaiser Hospital in Richmond and later in private practice in nearby Berkeley.

As her patient base and experience grew, she began to observe a consistent difference between those who recovered quickly from their injuries and those who did not.

Sara Webb, who would eventually become the executive director of the Rosen Institute, Marion's global training organization, explained it this way:

> When she worked on patients by hand, Marion would also talk to them, ask questions. Why did this happen to you? How do you feel about this or that?
>
> There was no particular point to begin with. She just had sort of a natural conversational style, and people felt comfortable confiding in her. But, over time, she began to realize that having people talk was one of the key factors in their getting and staying better.

Albeit unwittingly, Marion was uncovering the foundation of the Rosen Method—an understanding that the body is affected by what we experience, not only by physical injury but by emotional impact as well; that a chronic problem in our back, neck, or shoulders, for example, may have a *psychosomatic* (mind-body) cause.

Relieve the physical symptom, then discern the emotional source, and the trouble may be resolved, once and for all.

In our conversation, Sara pointed out:

> You have to understand that Marion was having these insights in the 1950s and 1960s, fairly early in the evolution of what is today accepted medical understanding. She was synthesizing what had so fascinated her as a young woman in Germany with her conventional training as a physical therapist.

She was bringing this knowledge to her clients. Among those who knew her, she had a reputation for relieving psychosomatic symptoms—things like chronic headache, tension, and back pain without an obvious physical cause. But she wasn't advertising it. There was no accepted venue for it at the time. . . . That was the problem.

It was a problem that would soon trigger a major crisis in Marion's life and, in time, generate her reinvention.

Midlife Turning Point

As she entered her mid-fifties, the scenario that had long worried Marion but that she had tried to ignore came to pass: the San Francisco area physicians who, for decades, had been her primary source of patient referrals began to retire or die off.

As her patient base dwindled, her professional practice—and with it, her life—dropped off a cliff.

The great joy she had experienced in her work—the flow—slowed to a trickle. The man she had married and the daughter she had raised were long gone. The money she had saved over the years was running low.

This gentle woman, who had provided so much relief to others, developed a chronic sense of tension and hopelessness that would not subside.

Like many of us whose careers are somehow derailed in life's second half, Marion found herself lost and alone in the proverbial dark wood (see Chapter 3). The dragons were circling, she told me, and there was no apparent way out:

I thought I would just wait it out until I got Social Security and sit down and wait until I died. That's what I thought would happen.

For quite some time, her thinking remained the same, including the moment when a much younger woman, filled with her own problems, telephoned Marion for help.

The caller was Sara Webb, then barely 22 years old. Sara had recently been fired from her position as an English teacher, her first job out of college.

As things turned out, it was a call that Marion would never forget:

Sara asked me if I could teach her what I had learned in Germany and included in my physical therapy work. Her brother, who suffered from asthma, had come to see me at one point, and in a few sessions, his asthma was gone. Sara's mother had told her to go see me and learn what I was doing. She thought maybe I could help Sara start a new career.[3]

At first, Marion's answer was a resounding no.

Shaken by her current circumstances, she had lost confidence in herself and her skills. Yes, she had been successful in treating patients, but what did she really know? She was no more than a physical therapist whose luck had run out.

And, even if she knew something special, she still spoke with a German accent and had no teaching experience.

Sara recalled the dialogue:

Marion said she couldn't teach anything, she had never taught anybody, and she wasn't willing to try. And then she called me back, the following day, and said she was willing to try if I wanted to, and we could just see how things worked out.

What happened between phone calls? Marion's memory about this remained vivid— she had had a long, soul-searching talk with herself:

This incident—Sara's contacting me—affected me deeply. She had gotten to me the same way I had gone to Lucy Heyer in Munich—her mother told her to do it. For me, this represented something I had put aside for 35 years, now emerging again in my life. When I decided to say yes to Sara, things started to change.

Marion was nearing her sixtieth birthday at the time of this decision, which ultimately would be the pivot point in the second half of her life—from personal crisis to yet untold potential and success.

Over the next several years, she reinvented herself into a masterful, much-in-demand teacher, and she pioneered therapeutic techniques that would, in time, be known and practiced around the world.

Looking back with her during our conversations, which took place when Marion was in her nineties, I wondered: Was there some lesson in the seemingly accidental way this all began?

Today, having a career fall apart after age 45 or 50 is increasingly commonplace. Not only do people lose or burn out in their jobs but many outlive their companies, or even entire industries that were flourishing when they first started out.

From Marion's experience, I asked, was there some message for those who find themselves in such a spot?

I think opening the door, opening your mind, makes all the difference. That's the important thing. You have to respond to the possibilities that life offers you. There's always something, you know, that can come your way. Something you can say yes to. So, see what comes your way, and say yes to it. And then follow it up.

Whatever happens to you, there are possibilities there. Maybe we just don't see them at first. Like in my case, you can say no, I can't teach, you know, I can't do that. Or you can say, well, I haven't tried. I haven't done that before.

And even now, I'm still doing that, all the time.

When people want me to give lectures in front of a hundred or two hundred or three hundred people—Wow—I can't speak in front of that many people. Yes, I can! I just have to open my mouth. And something might be coming out that other people might like to hear. Sometimes, it's not so interesting to me, maybe. But somebody back there in the corner thinks it was wonderful, it changed their life. For that, it's worth it!

We should just respond to whatever shows up. Because you can never tell what will show up next.

New Powers Emerge

What showed up in the process of Marion's reinvention were the three key elements we've seen in other personal reinventions:

Fascination: Taking on students allowed Marion to pursue what had fascinated her since her early twenties: the illusive connection between body and mind.

107

Flow: As her training business grew, so did the opportunities to do what she loved most: treat and relieve patients of their pain.

Structure for success: Along with Sara Webb and others, Marion ultimately created the Rosen Institute to provide a long-term economic and organizational structure for their mutual success.

But in achieving these things, something more emerged as well: Marion observed within herself *multiple new abilities and intelligences at work.*

She discovered that she *knew things* (crystallized intelligence), that she *knew how to invent ideas and solutions* (creative intelligence), and that she *knew how to teach and relate to people* (social intelligence) in ways that she had not previously been aware of.

In the next chapter, we'll examine how and why these developments—these remarkable manifestations of *innate wisdom and mastery*—can become available to each of us in life's second half.

Marion described her personal experience like this:

I became aware of knowing really much more than I had ever let out. When I was teaching Sara early on, sometimes she would watch while I worked on someone who came in. And I would touch that person in a way that they relaxed and started telling me things they had never said to anyone before. And that would help them get better and feel more alive.

And later Sara would ask: Why did that happen? In the beginning I didn't think it was because of anything I knew or *could explain. But when I looked further, I started to find research, new science that described what was happening, what happens in the body when you hold back, chemically, physically, and all of this.**

These things excited me and let me see why the things I had been doing had been effective. And all of sudden, when I became conscious of this information, it opened even more new ways of working and thinking. So, this is how my teaching, and the entire Rosen Method, developed over time.

What developed, along with this, was a large following, the likes of which Marion and Sara could never have foreseen.

Through Sara's social network, the word about Marion's work, and Sara's training, began to spread. Soon, new patients seeking treatment, more than either of them could handle, started to appear. Some—including career psychotherapists, physical therapists, and dancers—asked to be trained in Marion's methods as well.

In 1980, at age 66, Marion established her first full-scale, formal training program. Twelve participants were chosen for an intensive two-year curriculum at the newly formed Rosen Institute. Among them was Marion's niece, Marion Mehr, who was visiting from Sweden and who soon became instrumental in launching the first Rosen Method center outside the United States.

Over time, training centers were established in every region of the United States and all over Western Europe, as well as in Australia, Israel, and Canada. In 1989, several years before

---

*During the 1970s and 1980s the growing field of psychosomatic medicine helped to confirm the value of Marion's methods. Research showed, for example, that being gently touched leads to the release of oxytocin, a hormone that relaxes both body and mind.

the collapse of the Soviet Union, a Rosen center was opened in Moscow, following a visit by Marion there.

A little over a decade later, there were some 2,000 Rosen Method practitioners worldwide, many of them personally trained by Marion. There were books, CDs, videos, and innumerable newspaper and magazine articles focusing on Marion's healing methods.

In 2008, the *Rosen Method International Journal* was established online as an outlet for in-depth professional papers, including new scientific findings that shed light on her remarkable work.

What You Bring Forth

Through all of this, Marion, with whom I visited three times in the process of writing this book, grew older, along with the rest of us.

When last I met with her, she was nearly 95. Her walk was a little less certain, but her energy remained boundless, and the twinkle in her eyes seemed brighter than ever.

On the wall of her modest office hung a quotation I couldn't help but notice:

If You Bring Forth What Is Within You, What You Bring Forth Will Save You.

If You Do Not Bring Forth What Is Within You, What You Do Not Bring Forth Will Destroy You.

What special significance did this hold for her? I asked.

I always feel when you have a potential, you really have to use it. We all have potential inside of us. Just look at me. When we are at the height of our knowledge and the height of our lives, why should we give that up? Why should we not use what we have gotten in 60, 70, 80, 90 years? And hand it on to where it is wanted? It seems ridiculous to me.

If you don't use your potential, it hits back at you. It strikes back, because it works on you, it wants to come out. And in order not to come out, you have to hold it back. And that is very bad for your health, very bad for your personality, very bad for your relationships. It doesn't work!

I know people who were active earlier in their lives and then have not done anything — they usually die off much earlier. And those of us who have been doing things, and doing different things, we seemed to have lived longer and have lived healthier lives.

My sister is four years younger than me, and she had to retire from her work in Stockholm at age 70. And she had known a lot about music, about poetry and other things. But somehow she doesn't use it, and she has a lot of physical complications. She has a lot of friends, and a son who loves her, and grandchildren who love her, but something is missing in her. And it's not missing in me.

I have only one grandson. I have friends, not famous or important people, just people. But I work. I give out what's in me, and I have very few physical complaints, very few. I have it as good as one can have it at my age.

In the final moments we spent together, Marion made a promise that hardly surprised me. She said she would never quit:

I would not want to live a retirement life. Living that way would be tragic. It's so wonderful to be my age and have experienced what I have and still be wanted—be asked to share it, and really have something to offer. To give that up—it's inconceivable. I'm just as happy to go on doing what I love to do until I really die. When I can't work anymore, I might consider dying.

chapter
seven

The Neuroscience of Potential

Why We're Hardwired to Reinvent

Our only purpose in life is to put up the best performance we can.
— Francis Chichester, winner of seven world records in sailing after age 65

I f they had a Hall of Fame for Whiz Kids in Silicon Valley, Steven Aldrich would surely be in it.

While still in the MBA program at Stanford, he co-founded the first big dot-com to link consumers with insurance companies for instant online rate quotes. Before the ink dried on his diploma, he sold his start-up to Intuit, the financial software giant, and walked away with an estimated $10 million.[1]

Asked *Stanford Business Bulletin*: "What's next for the 29-year-old alum who seems to have fit an entire career into his first months out of business school?"[2] After a series of corporate posts, Steven delivered an answer: he signed on with a small company on the cutting edge of one of the hottest topics in twenty-first-century science: *the lifelong potential of the human mind.*

113

When I spoke with Steven, he was about a year into his new role as CEO of San Francisco-based Posit Science, Inc., a pioneer in the field of brainware—software designed to enhance cognitive performance.

I asked if he was even aware that this field existed before he got into it:

> *I wasn't, and I think that was one of the really captivating reasons that led me to want to become part of it. Once I saw what was possible, and I studied the demographic shifts—not just in the United States but worldwide, toward the graying of the population—I connected the dots. And what was clear was that Posit Science had a line of products that could be very impactful in peoples' lives, and it could be a very big business if we played our cards right.*
>
> *It's been an amazing time of discovery for me personally.*

I soon came to appreciate his excitement —and to be astonished at the remarkable potential for reinvention that has only recently been revealed within the three pounds of gelatinous material that we call the human brain.

The Next "New, New Thing"

I reached out to Steven Aldrich and a range of others in the brain science area when I found myself increasingly bothered by a question as I was writing this book:

**What was going on with the reinventive people
I was encountering?**

People like Marion Rosen and Shep Nuland—individuals who had seen unexpected talents and capabilities suddenly emerge, from within, in midlife and beyond? Were they special cases? Had they drunk from some secret fountain of youth?

For that matter, what about people like architect Frank Lloyd Wright, choreographer Martha Graham, poet Stanley Kunitz, heart surgeon Michael DeBakey, folk artist Grandma Moses, Supreme Court Justice Oliver Wendell Holmes, and the Greek playwright Sophocles, who all produced remarkable work *at or after the age of 90?*

Were they all aberrations? Or was there something inside these prolific individuals that the rest of us might have as well?

As I dug into these puzzles, I began to see what excellent company I shared: I discovered that these were precisely the issues that had lately come to fascinate the superstars of neuroscience—the neurosurgeons, neurobiologists, and neuropsychologists who were among the thought leaders in their fields in the United States and around the globe.

Indeed, the conclusion they had reached, only in recent years, was that *much if not most of what they, and we, had always believed about lifelong mental capabilities was worse than flat-out wrong.*

Where it had long been considered inarguable that the normal brain, like other human organs, was fated to wear out over time—to lose its resilience and ability to function, to stumble over what it already knows—on the leading edge of twenty-first-century neuroscience, a radically different picture had emerged.

"Recently, powerful methods of functional neuroimaging became available, and they revolutionized brain research," New York University (NYU) clinical neurology professor Elkhonon

Goldberg reported in 2005. "The impact of neuroimaging has been likened to the impact of the telescope on astronomy. All of a sudden . . . high-tech terms like PET, fMRI, and SPECT, . . . they all give us a direct window into the activity of the working brain."[3]

Through this new window what became clear, according to neuropsychiatrist Richard Restak, is that "the brain of an older person is not inferior to that of a younger counterpart; instead, the brain of an 80-year-old is *organized* differently. In practical terms this means the mature brain possesses strengths and assets that it lacked decades earlier."[4]

These new strengths may allow for "the discharge of very high level professional and executive responsibilities and even world-class feats of artistic and scientific creativity and statesmanship," added NYU's Goldberg, pointing out that "history is replete with examples of great creative genius and political leadership reaching its peak only at the age of 60, 70, and even 80. Scientists commonly refer to this mysterious ability as 'cognitive expertise' and its mechanisms have for years remained obscure."[5]

Until now.

Let me underscore the significance of all of this in the context of our conversation in this book:

State-of-the art neuroscience has determined that the human brain was never designed for decline or retirement but for continual reinvention and success.

In fact, extraordinary powers become available to us in the second half of life that were not available in the first.

As we will see in this chapter and the next, the mature brain, when properly maintained, has the potential to be continually transformed—to draw upon and synthesize its vast storage banks of knowledge and experience in ways that can be downright startling.

Here's just one example.

How Fast Can You Spell Backward?

In 1996, at the age of 101, Anna Morgan of Rehoboth, Massachusetts, was asked by researchers if she would donate her brain to science. "But I'm still using it," was her reply.

And that she was: in the same maverick ways that she had all of her life.

In her thirties, Anna distributed condoms for birth control, years before their use was fully legal. In her forties, she organized workers during the Great Depression. In her late sixties, during the McCarthy hearings era, she was found guilty of contempt for refusing to testify before the Ohio State Committee on Un-American Activities—a ruling later overturned by the U.S. Supreme Court.

"I had a very healthy contempt for the committee," she said.

In her nineties, she wrote some 1,200 pages of memoirs, worked successfully to have a new postage stamp issued, and volunteered for numerous human rights groups. On her one hundredth birthday, she testified before the U.S. Congress.[6]

Accomplishments such as these attracted the attention of brain scientists conducting the famous New England Centenarian Study. But it was Anna's neurological test results *after* such late life mental challenges that completely blew them away.

Their exam notes read like this: "To this day, our fellow neuropsychologists gasp when they see videotape of Ms. Morgan repeating the details of a story she had heard only minutes before, with practically no hesitation and few errors. Even after having told the story hundreds of times, we ourselves have difficulty recalling all its details. It impressed us that, even at 101 years old, someone could perform better on some of the most demanding cognitive tests than the people administering them."[7]

Researchers tried every functional experiment they knew. And, with each state-of-the-art check, Anna disproved the notion that getting older necessarily meant losing the potential of the brain.

On sustained attention experiments, she repeated seven-digit number strings flawlessly. She could hear five-digit number strings and repeat them backward with ease. She spelled words in reverse, counted backward from 20, and recited the alphabet rapidly. When her abstract reasoning and conceptual skills were challenged, as in every other case, she performed as though she were 40 years younger than her age.

As they wrapped up their neurological tests, Anna told researchers that she was planning to make all her own funeral arrangements before anything happened to her. "I don't want my children to be burdened with all this detail," she said, "They're old, you know."[8]

Still shaking their heads, her highly credentialed inquisitors wrote: "Anna Morgan had no signs of dementia, and in our estimation, was as engaged in and enthusiastic about life as a high school sophomore."[9]

When Anna finally did pass away, at age 102, the experts remained perplexed.

Today, however, they understand.

Talk about a Revolution!

Through many decades, it was considered an immutable fact, by scientists as well as laypeople, that, by the age of 2 or 3, we're in possession of all the brain cells we'll ever have. It was also believed that, over time, the accumulated loss of brain cells will inevitably catch up with us.

Just before the close of the twentieth century, scientists discovered that this just wasn't so.

Here's what they found, instead: while the average mature brain generally processes information more slowly and less accurately than a younger model and is more vulnerable to disease, it continues to generate new neurons (brain cells) from "cradle to grave," through a process called *neurogenesis*.

And there's more: *the most significant factor influencing this process, as well as our overall mental performance, is how—and whether—we use the brain we have.*

Our understanding of this last phenomenon is due largely to a California neuroscientist named Michael Merzenich, known for his assertion that "contemporary neuroscience is revealing, for the first time in our history, our true human nature."[10]

In 2003, Merzenich was among those who founded Posit Science, Inc., the brain development software firm mentioned at the beginning of this chapter.

Several years before, it was his revolutionary experiments "mapping" the brains of monkeys and, later, learning-disabled children, that allowed him to sell the neuroscience world on a revolutionary notion: with use, the brain can be continually modified and molded. He called this phenomenon *neuroplasticity*.

"Let me tell you what happened when I began to declare that the brain was plastic. I received hostile treatment,"

Merzenich told an interviewer. "I got people saying things in reviews such as: 'This would be really interesting if it could possibly be true, but it could not be.' It was as if I just made it up."[11]

But his science was so solid that the skeptics soon came to acknowledge that he was right: neuroplasticity was a breakthrough of enormous scale.

"Before Merzenich's work," wrote Norman Doidge, a research psychiatrist at Columbia University, "the brain was seen as a complex machine, having unalterable limits on memory, processing speed, and intelligence." Merzenich proved "that each of these assumptions is wrong. In a series of brilliant experiments he showed that the shape of our brain maps changes depending upon what we do over the course of our lives."[12]

Work It or Lose It

What Merzenich demonstrated is that the things we learn and do literally "remap" our mental real estate and that the brain is in a continual state of flux—of plasticity—recalibrating, resculpting, and rewiring itself in response to our life experiences.

If, as we get older, we put our mental gears into idle, our brain will accommodate itself to inaction: its agility, speed, and accuracy will fall off, and its full, lifetime potential will be diminished or lost.

The main reason, Merzenich explained, "is that it is not being appropriately exercised. We have an intense period of learning in childhood. Every day is a day of new stuff. And then, in our early employment, we are intensely engaged in learning and acquiring new skills and abilities."[13]

It's this kind of rigorous activity that grows the brain and allows it to evolve. That transformation, in turn, can generate enhanced performance and capabilities, no matter what our age.

Simply put, our brains work best when they are worked hard.

Additionally, neuroscientists have increasingly come to believe that intense mental work may help protect us from, or at least slow, the development of brain disorders and diseases, including Alzheimer's.

That said, as life goes on, the continuation of hard, challenging work is generally not "the program" we follow. Geoff Colvin, an expert in human performance, states the obvious: "Most people stop the deliberate practice necessary to sustain their performance; . . . they've decided to stop pushing it."

A relative few, on the other hand, "manage to continue achieving at high levels well beyond the point where age-related declines would seem to make that impossible."[14]

The deciding factor? How we choose to use the brains that we've been given and invest our time.

> **As in life's first half, men and women who achieve big things in midlife and beyond put their minds to it.**

Anna Morgan, the high-performance 100-plus-year-old, clearly made the choice to "keep pushing it." She continued challenging her brain, leveraging its natural plasticity throughout her life.

But, as we are about to see, remarkable as they may have been, the functions of speed, accuracy, and agility that Anna demonstrated in her neurological exams are only part of the mature mind's story.

As we grow older, powerful capabilities that are far less understood become available to us as well.

Higher Order in the Court

When Justice William Brennan retired from the U.S. Supreme Court, at age 84, it was due to physical health issues—the intellectual demands of the job were no problem at all. During his 34 years on the bench, Brennan wrote an astounding 1,200 opinions and was forever on the prowl for the next challenging case.

Shortly before Brennan reluctantly stepped down, his biographer, Stephen Vermiel, described him this way:

▶ JUSTICE BRENNAN is continually using his mind on something that is an absolute passion to him. The man keeps growing. Otherwise, an 83-year-old veteran of World War II wouldn't be defending your right to burn the flag.

Discussing cases, it's amazing how crisply he sees things. Maybe because he knows what the cases are really about, he isn't so concerned with irrelevant details. I'll study the case, ask him about this angle, that angle, and it's not that complicated to him. He certainly seems to see the cases more clearly than his law clerks, young hotshots though they may be. One hundred seven law clerks in 33 years![15]

Well into his eighties, Brennan could see through the intricate fog of law more clearly than legal eagles from Harvard, Yale, and Stanford law schools who were many decades younger.

How could this be possible?

Not far from the marble edifice where the Supreme Court conducts its business, I sat down with a Harvard-trained alchemist for whom it was not in the least bit a surprise.

The Wisdom Doctor

Bow-tied, bespectacled, and spry, Gene Cohen, MD, PhD, was in his early sixties when we met. Highly accomplished, yet modest and unassuming, he exhibited many of the character traits commonly associated with that legendary state of mind called *wisdom*—a subject he'd been investigating through the entirety of his career.

For nearly five centuries, since the Sumerians first etched into clay their notion that unique capabilities accrue with age, theologians and philosophers have debated these questions: Does wisdom really exist? And if so, where does it come from, and what is it?[16]

Recently, such inquiries have become fertile territory for scientific analysis, with neurobiologists, sociologists, and research psychologists from highly respected institutions digging in.

But with his in-depth studies of more than 3,000 older men and women, compiled over multiple decades, Dr. Gene Cohen, a pioneer in the field of maturity, laid claim to the scientific underpinnings of wisdom long before the rest of the pack appeared.

We spoke in his office at George Washington University, where he was a distinguished professor of psychiatry and founding director of the Center on Aging, Health & Humanities.

> *Q: When you hear about someone like Supreme Court Justice William Brennan who, at age 83, is running circles around some of the best legal minds in the country, you don't think that's an aberration?*
>
> *A: No, not at all. For so long, when an older person has done something interesting or positive, people have said, "Wow, they did that despite their age." What my work is*

showing is that many of these things are happening not despite aging but because of it!

Q: *How did you arrive at that conclusion?*

A: *I study the brain science, in a biological sense, that's going on among my colleagues—the new findings from brain imaging and so forth. At the same time, my own research has been on psychological development in older people. And I've been looking at how those areas link together.*

As we now know, through this whole new understanding of brain neuroplasticity, every time we challenge our brain, we modify it. What my research has shown is that, over time, that subtle modification helps to alter the way we think, feel, and act.

Q: *So you're proposing that this thing we call wisdom emerges as the result of those modifications in the brain?*

A: *No, not entirely. I don't see biology alone as the cause, but it's contributory. It's a part of the equation.*

Wisdom, Gene asserted, is what psychologists call a *developmental product*, a synergy of brain biology, maturity, and life experience that ripens over time. "These things can't be bought, and they can't be rushed," he once wrote, "so it is not surprising that wisdom, though not unique to later life, is associated more often with aging."[17]

Brain Changes + Maturity + Experience = Wisdom

And while wisdom's manifestation in each of us, individually, is neither automatic nor assured, the potential exists for nearly everyone.

> *wis'dom: Quality of being wise; ability to judge soundly and deal sagaciously with facts, especially as they relate to life and conduct; knowledge, with the capacity to make due use of it; perception of the best ends and the best means; discernment and judgment; discretion; sagacity.*
>
> *— Webster's Third New International Dictionary,*
> *Seventh Edition, Merriam-Webster, 2000*

We're Gonna Be in the Hudson

On January 15, 2009, less than two minutes after takeoff from New York's LaGuardia International Airport, U.S. Airways Flight 1549, loaded with 155 passengers and crew, struck a large flock of geese that knocked out both of its engines over America's most populous city.

"It was the worst, sickening, pit-of-your-stomach, falling-through-the-floor feeling I've ever felt in my life," said 58-year-old Captain Chesley Sullenberger. "I immediately knew it was very bad."[18]

As his 81-ton aircraft began to fall from the sky, its cabin filling with the smell of burning birds, Sullenberger's decades as an Air Force fighter pilot, commercial captain, and aviation safety instructor kicked in: "The physiological reaction I had was strong, and I had to force myself to use my training and force calm on the situation."

Sullenberger took control from the first officer, Jeffrey Skiles, declaring: "My aircraft." And, as air traffic controllers desperately searched for an emergency runway somewhere in the area, Sullenberger conducted a lightning fast analysis and radioed in his decision: "We're gonna be in the Hudson."

Within moments, "Sully," as he was known, instructed the passengers to "brace for impact," and he glided the powerless Airbus 320 onto the frigid surface of the Hudson River near Midtown Manhattan. "Despite the sky-high odds against a successful water landing," reported the *New York Times*, everyone aboard survived.

"Miracle on the Hudson," pronounced New York's governor. "Grace under pressure," proclaimed *Time* magazine.[19]

Naturally reserved and reticent to accept the hero status that was showered upon him, Sullenberger's own interpretation was this: "For 42 years, I've been making small, regular deposits in this bank of experience, education, and training. And on January 15 the balance was sufficient so that I could make a very large withdrawal."[20]

Observing Captain Sullenberger, students of the brain, like Dr. Gene Cohen, would have smiled in agreement and summed it all up with two words: *cognitive template*.

"Wisdom is made up of multiple forms of intelligence," Gene told me during our visit. "It is a mature integration of thinking, creativity, and social or emotional intellect."

Like an internal "board of directors," these forms of intelligence may operate individually or collectively on a given challenge or situation. What's more, neuroscientists believe that each of wisdom's three components has its own physical "seat" or location within the brain:

▶ The Trilogy of Wisdom

Crystallized intelligence

Creative intelligence

Emotional and Social intelligence

In Captain Sullenberger's case, it was primarily his *crystallized intelligence—the experience, knowledge, and reason* component of wisdom—that was triggered into play.

As his aircraft plummeted from the sky, there was no time to think. Even a much younger and faster mind could not likely have calculated all possible scenarios and made the accurate split-second judgment call that Sullenberger did.

Instead, his 58-year-old brain went into literal "mental autopilot." Neuroscientists observing him, with brain imaging technology, would have watched for the left hemisphere of his cerebral cortex to "light up," indicating ignition of what they call *cognitive templates*, or templates of crystallized expertise.

Technically, these are networks of neurons that rapidly search the brain's long-term memory, seeking patterns between what's happening in the moment, what's happened to us in the past, and what the future might be. From that computation, our brain "intuits" or "pops up" with a solution to our current emergency or predicament.

The experience feels like confidently "knowing exactly what to do."

That this process of "mining our experience" for "earlier similars" can occur instantaneously within the brain of a jet pilot, careening into all-but-certain disaster, speaks to its extraordinary power.

127

Nobel laureate Herbert Simon and others have asserted that cognitive templates are among the most critical, if not the foremost, mechanisms of higher-order thinking. But they are not easy to come by. Cognitive templates are the rewards of experience, an aspect of our long-term crystallized intelligence that is seared into the brain solely by accumulated real life.[21]

Chesley Sullenberger had logged some 19,000 hours in the cockpit before his "miracle" on the Hudson. His military training included crisis simulations including, most likely, emergency water landings. He earned his cognitive templates along with his captain's stripes.

The same can be said for Supreme Court Justice William Brennan's striking ability, in the ninth decade of life, to cut to the chase through irrelevant details and "see the cases more clearly" than could those around him, no matter how complex the issues may have been.

Experience does matter; and it can have a positive impact well beyond the professions or businesses with which we've been most directly involved over the years.

For one thing, neuroscientists are discovering that, along with superior problem-solving abilities, experienced knowledge workers may bring to their later years an extra "coat of mental armor" against some of the natural neural erosion that generally accompanies age.[22]

Furthermore, and exceptionally relevant to our conversation on reinvention in midlife and beyond, it is also now known that we mold our own mental templates.

Templates of Experience Transfer from One Success to Another

As we've seen in previous chapters, years of know-how in one area can provide the foundation for reinventing one's success in another, seemingly distinct field.

Is not an experienced pilot a trained crisis manager? The great professor, a skilled persuader? The successful courtroom lawyer, an educator? The winning sales manager, a coach? The journalist, a novelist? The corporate executive, a negotiator? The movie actor, a politician (in some cases, literally)?

Although we may not realize it at times, the experiences—the challenges faced and met—that you and I carry with us, from the first half of life into the rest, are, in a real and neurologically measurable sense, incomparable gifts that form the basis of our crystallized intelligence, one of the three main ingredients of wisdom.

The Debate over Creativity

Like other fields of scientific exploration, modern neuroscience has evolved, and continues to do so, through a process of findings and, quite frequently, fights.

We saw earlier that Michael Merzenich had to argue over his concept of neuroplasticity before it was widely accepted by colleagues at the turn of the twenty-first century.

At about the same time, Dr. Gene Cohen found himself in a heated debate with fellow brain experts over another controversial topic: the area of *creative intelligence,* the human potential to invent new things and ideas.

Over the years, much has been documented in neuroscience journals about the young geniuses—the scientists, inventors, artists, writers, designers, composers—whose achievements, in their twenties and thirties had, throughout history, animated life and world culture.

But far less has been said of older masters who, quite successfully, reinvented their work. And hardly a fraction of attention had ever been paid to men and women who might be called *late and unexpected bloomers*—people who surprisingly uncovered significant creative capacities in midlife and beyond.

We've already visited with several such individuals, and we've seen how their talents emerged: Shep Nuland, the career surgeon unpredictably turned bestselling author, and Marion Rosen, the physical therapist who found, within herself, world-class teaching and entrepreneurial skills. In the chapters ahead, we'll meet with other reinventive people, including a hardened district attorney whose unknown photographic genius appeared to him, quite literally, from out of the blue.

How does creative intelligence like this suddenly appear? Why has this phenomenon so rarely been acknowledged?

Is this too an aspect of wisdom—a gift of life's second half?

Dr. Gene Cohen adamantly believed so. In fact, over many decades of studying human development, no area of inquiry was of keener interest to him. And nothing aggravated, or provoked, him more than the reluctance of others in his field to focus on it.

During our conversation, he told me:

The idea that we grow as we grow older, that creativity can emerge or continue to develop, goes against what is widely considered popular wisdom or common sense. When I speak at professional conferences, I'm constantly challenged about it. I call them "gotcha" questions because they are usually raised by people who sincerely believe they have evidence that contradicts mine.

Mild mannered as he was, I found Gene's pitched battle with other brain scientists about the roots of creativity to be quite surprising—and I asked him to elaborate on it.

Q: Why do you suppose your colleagues argue with you?

A: The historian Daniel Boorstin once said, "The greatest obstacle to discovery is not ignorance; it's the illusion of knowledge." In the field of aging, for years many people had the illusion that there was nothing to be learned. So they didn't study it, and not studying it confirmed their illusion.

One of the challenges I hear most often has to do with career achievement and the observation that the greatest accomplishments of humankind's best and brightest typically occurred early in their careers. At first glance, that might seem true. But it's only part of the human story.

Q: What's the rest?

A: That creativity and the potential for creative thinking later in life were always there. When you look back over the centuries, you see people like Socrates, Copernicus, and Galileo, but there were many other people who also did remarkable things in their later years. Yet, compared to younger creators, their numbers appear small because so few people lived into old age.

In the United States, for instance, in the year 1900 life expectancy was still under 50. And it's only in the second half of the twentieth century that the numbers of older people began to grow. But the misconceptions and negative stereotypes about aging have become so ingrained in our culture that even the experts have failed to see an accurate picture.

As part of his debate with colleagues, Gene penned an entire book on the subject: *The Creative Age: Awakening Human Potential in the Second Half of Life*. In it, he included hundreds of examples of creative achievement among older people, and he pointed to the newly emerging neuroscience behind it.

Said Gene:

There's now a whole field of research called "post-formal thinking," which is an evolution, a breakthrough in the way we view intellectual development. Developmental pioneers like Jean Piaget used to think that pure analytical thought was the final stage, the highest order of our human intellect. Piaget thought that maturity meant thinking like a scientist.

We now know that's not true.

We have come to understand that, as we get older, our intellectual development continues. It grows into a type of thinking that is not just objective, but subjective — into a type of thinking that doesn't just look for the answer but recognizes that there may be competing solutions.

It is this new level of flexible thinking that is the key to enhanced personal creativity and innovation in midlife and beyond.

We begin to perceive the world in new ways. And as I was studying all of this, I began to think: it's almost as if the left brain and the right brain are becoming more integrated. And about that same time, in 2002, new research came out from Duke University. What the neuroscientists there found, by using brain imaging to study different people at different ages, is pretty much what I had begun to suspect.

Prior to middle age, for any given task, we use one side of the brain more than the other. We use the left brain for certain tasks, the right for others. But when we hit middle age, we begin to use both sides together. Technically, it's called "bilateral hemisphere involvement." This is the source of the development of "post-formal thinking," later in life, on an anatomical level.

It's as if we move into all-wheel drive, as if the heart and the mind come together!

Further research has since underscored the Duke University studies and Gene Cohen's thinking. Through new imaging technology, neuroscientists have become increasingly microspecific about the functions of the brain's various regions, including the working of its information processing center, the cerebral cortex:

Cerebral cortex

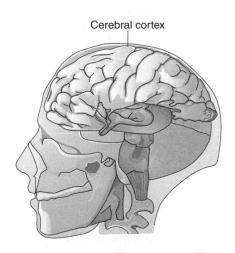

And while brain experts rarely agree completely on anything, there is general concurrence on this: the left hemisphere of the cerebral cortex is the repository of our logical reasoning skills along with our *crystallized intelligence*, which includes long-term knowledge and know-how (*cognitive templates*), whereas the right side is the "novelty" hemisphere, home to our intuitive operations and *fluid intelligence*, including the capacity to learn, absorb, and manage new information, problems, and experiences.[23]

Left brain   Right brain

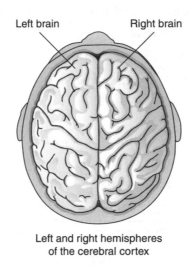

Left and right hemispheres
of the cerebral cortex

Separately, these hemispheres are the building blocks of human intellect. Working together, they form, with a reasonable degree of certainty, the foundation for creative wisdom in life's second half.

Emotional Intelligence

"The highest form of wisdom is kindness," declares the ancient Hebrew text, the Talmud.

What about character traits like kindness, generosity, patience, or other attributes commonly ascribed to wise women and men? Is there credible evidence that personal qualities like these actually emerge later in life? Or is this just the stuff of legend and Hollywood screenplays?

Consider this scenario.

There's a moment early in the movie *Gran Torino* when the audience braces for the worst. It's the first of several times when 78-year-old Walt Kowalski—an embittered, racist Korean War veteran—reaches for his M1 rifle.

"Yeah, I blow a hole in your face," snarls the recently widowed, former auto assembly worker, "and I go back in the house and I sleep like a baby. You can count on that."[24]

There's a lot you can rely on in the film, which first reached theaters in 2009.

You can depend on Clint Eastwood, who plays the main character, to embody the resentment Kowalski feels as his formerly white, working-class Detroit neighborhood becomes a violence-ridden ghetto, dominated by poor Asian immigrants.

You can taste Kowalski's rage when Thao, the teenage son of the Hmong (Southeast Asian) family next door, attempts to steal his beloved 1972 Ford Gran Torino, as part of a gang initiation rite.

But you cannot easily anticipate what comes next: how, in the face of deeply felt apologies from Thao's sister and family, Walt Kowalski's hard edge softens; the way he begins to understand, for the first time in his long years, that people of every race and color suffer equally in the search for meaning and love.

Confronting his unexplored disappointments and failures, Walt Kowalski is transformed from his neighbors' enemy into their protector. And, ultimately, it is on their behalf that he lays down his life.

"The message of the story is great," said Eastwood, who, nearing age 80, was also the movie's director and producer. "It shows you're never too old to learn," he explained, "whether it's tolerance or anything else."[25]

Sounds truly wonderful. But how much of this is really so?

Do we become emotionally and socially wiser in life's second half?

In the 1980s and 1990s this became an inquiry of significant interest at leading neuroscience research centers across America. The consensus that has since emerged is a resounding yes.

At Stanford University, for example, decades of research by Dr. Laura Carstensen, director of the Longevity Center, has shown "that older people seem to have figured out how to manage their emotions in a profoundly important way."[26]

The manifestations of this emotional regulation are varied and wide ranging. Compared with younger people, numerous studies have indicated that older men and women are demonstrably:

- More resilient and even keeled
- Better able to deal with ambiguity
- More compassionate and empathetic
- Better able to determine what's important
- Superior at negotiating solutions
- More skillful at managing crises

The implications of such findings are far reaching. They suggest, for example, that given the opportunities, 60- to 70-year-olds might have significant strategic advantages over younger men and women in situations that require careful deliberation amid competing points of view—including positions in leadership, management, planning, labor relations, public affairs, and conflict resolution.

And, as it further challenges societal typecasting, another striking piece of research seems worth pointing out here: as we mature, we grow quantifiably *happier and more optimistic*, on average, than people half our age. This has been consistently documented in a variety of settings and situations, inside the laboratory and out.

"There is a split between reality and perception," explains Dr. Carstensen. "I call it the *misery myth*. People expect to become less happy as they grow older, yet our studies show that the frequency that one feels sad and angry declines. And when negative emotions do occur, they don't last as long."[27]

The Gifts of Wisdom

Are these shifts in personality and perspective the result of life experiences or of fundamental changes in brain structure?

As with the other components of wisdom we've looked at, the answer is: a combination of both.

Of late, some neuroscientists have focused considerable attention on the so-called emotional centers of the brain, most especially the *amygdala*, the almond-shaped structure in the brain's limbic system that is commonly referred to as "the seat of fight or flight."

There is growing evidence that age has a natural calming effect on amygdala function—that we become much less likely to emotionally "snap" or suffer what experts call *amygdala hijackings* as the years go by.

Elsewhere, brain scientists are scrutinizing another set of clues to emotional maturity. As of this writing, a new set of studies is underway at Duke University's Center for Cognitive Neuroscience.

There, the objective is to investigate noted disparities in the ways younger and older brains process and store negative input, to determine how these variations might impact mood and mindset.[28]

Whatever the anatomical verdicts, one thing is increasingly agreed upon: our temperament and perspective can, in significant ways, be reborn as we mature.

The character of the iconic elder—the sage capable of perceiving what others cannot, of remaining calm in a storm, of rendering a unique brand of creative solutions to seemingly intractable problems—is not simply a figment of myth, movies, or fairy tales.

It's the real thing.

Indeed, the potential for all three components of wisdom we've examined—advanced emotional intelligence, enhanced creativity, and the power of crystallized experience—seems to be hardwired into us, with a time-release mechanism calibrated for life's second half.

Throughout history, wise men and women have leveraged and celebrated this human asset. Long before the brain scientists could prove it, they appear to have known, instinctively, that as we grow older, we grow more powerful, not less.

And no matter the naysayers, obstacles, or social stereotypes, they've used their inborn gifts to discover their full potential and reinvent their success.

From Age 90 to 100

At 100, composer Elliot Carter celebrated his birthday with a concert at Carnegie Hall that included 40 musical works he had written since age 90.

At 100, Grandma Moses (Anna Mary Robertson), one of America's foremost folk artists, was still painting. She generated over 3,600 canvasses from the time she started painting in her seventies until her death at age 101.

At 96, Martha Graham, the pioneer of modern dance, choreographed her last complete ballet, Maple Leaf Rag. She personally performed on stage until age 76.

At 95, Nobel laureate Dr. Rita Levi-Montalcini established a neuroscience research institute in Rome and oversaw its work until her death at 100.

At 93, Dr. Marguerite Voit, whose earlier work helped explain why some viruses can lead to cancer, continued her groundbreaking cell biology research at the Salk Institute in San Diego.

At 92, Dr. George W. Comstock, regarded by his peers as the world's foremost expert on tuberculosis, oversaw community-based research on cancer and heart disease at the Johns Hopkins Center for Public Health Research.

At 91, famed architect Frank Lloyd Wright completed his design of the Guggenheim Museum in New York. At the same age, legendary cellist Pablo Casals was asked why he continued to practice. "Because I am making progress," was his reply.

At 90, Sophocles wrote Oedipus at Colonus. He penned his masterpiece Oedipus Rex, on which Freud based his pioneering psychoanalytic theory, at age 71.

At 90, Merce Cunningham, the legendary choreographer, debuted his latest work, Nearly Ninety, *at the Brooklyn Academy of Music.*

In his mid-nineties, Daniel Schorr, the last of Edward R. Murrow's CBS news team, continued broadcasting commentary and analysis on National Public Radio. "I never expected to be working now," he told USA Today, *"but I'll take it."*

In his nineties, agricultural scientist Norman Borlaug, whose earlier work in food production saved hundreds of millions of lives, marshaled efforts to tackle a new variety of rust that threatened the world's wheat supplies.

At 90, Oliver Wendell Holmes, known as "the great dissenter," was still writing landmark law on the Supreme Court. He was first appointed to the court at age 61.

At 90, Albert Schweitzer continued working at his hospital at Lamaberene, after receiving the Nobel Peace Prize, at age 77, for his missionary work in Africa.

At age 90, Dr. Michael DeBakey, inventor of the artificial heart, ceased performing heart surgery to concentrate on laboratory research and cardiac postoperative care, work he continued until his death at age 99.

From Their Mid-Seventies through Late Eighties

At 88, Michelangelo was still at work on St. Peter's Basilica in the Vatican. He was appointed architect of St. Peter's, the cathedral of the popes, at age 72.

At 87, sculptor Louise Bourgeois created Spider, *which sold at auction for more than $4 million, one of the highest prices ever paid for the work of a living sculptor.*

In their late eighties, TV correspondent Mike Wallace and commentator Andy Rooney continued broadcasting on 60 Minutes, *the top-rated weekly news program.*

In his mid-eighties, Sumner Redstone remained at the helm as executive chairman of Viacom, Inc., and the CBS Corporation.

At 84, Susan B. Anthony, the social reformer, founded the International Woman Suffrage Alliance in Berlin.

At 83, Johann Wolfgang von Goethe finished the second part of his epic play Faust, *one of the most important works in German literature.*

At 82, Kurt Vonnegut, the novelist, playwright, poet, and essayist, published A Man Without a Country, *another of his many bestsellers.*

In his early eighties, pioneering nuclear chemist Gerhard Friedlander of the Manhattan Project returned to Brookhaven National Laboratories to work on the famous Gallex experiment.

At 81, satirist Art Buchwald continued to publish his syndicated newspaper column. He once wrote that he favored pastries over exercise, which he considered dangerous to his health.

At 80, Giuseppe Verdi completed his comic opera Falstaff, *widely considered one of the finest operas ever written.*

At 79, William Carlos Williams, the pediatrician and poet, pub-lished Pictures from Bruegel, *which was awarded the Pulitzer Prize.*

At 79, Katherine Graham, the publisher, wrote her first book, Personal History, *which won a Pulitzer Prize.*

At 78, Benjamin Franklin invented the first bifocal eyeglasses to help correct his own vision. He was 70 when he helped draft the Declaration of Independence.

At 78, Bertrand Russell, mathematician and philosopher, was awarded the Nobel Prize for Literature. He later wrote his Autobiography *between ages 95 and 97.*

In their late seventies, Warren Buffett was running Berkshire Hathaway and Rupert Murdoch was still leading News Corporation.

At 77, Mahatma Gandhi completed negotiations for Britain to grant independence to India, and Albert Schweitzer won the Nobel Peace Prize for his missionary work in Africa.

At 77, Winston Churchill became prime minister of England for the second time. He won the Nobel Prize for Literature at 79.

At 76, biologist Benjamin Duggar discovered Aureomycin, the antibiotic "wonder drug" that killed off bacterial infections no other drug could cure.

From Their Mid-Sixties to Mid-Seventies

At 75, Nelson Mandela, four years after being released from nearly three decades in prison, was elected president of South Africa, a post he held until age 80.

At 74, architect Antoni Gaudi was considered to be at the peak of his creativity, working on his famous cathedral in Barcelona, when he was killed in an auto accident.

Until age 76, Golda Meir was still prime minister of Israel. She was first elected at age 70.

At 73, George C. Marshall was awarded the Nobel Peace Prize for the famous Marshall Plan, which he developed in his late sixties, while serving as U.S. secretary of state.

At 73, Alfred North Whitehead published A History of Western Philosophy.

At 72, Carl Sandburg was awarded a Pulitzer Prize for publication of his Complete Poems. *He continued to write into his late eighties.*

At 72, Israeli Prime Minister Yitzhak Rabin, Israeli Foreign Minister Shimon Perez (age 71), and PLO Chairman Yasser Arafat (age 65) won the 1994 Nobel Peace Prize for their courage in carrying out backdoor peace negotiations in the Middle East.

Into his seventies, Thomas Edison headed the Naval Consulting Board, directing research on antisubmarine warfare and technology. At 65, he had produced the first talking motion pictures.

At 71, Phineas Barnum cofounded the famous Barnum and Bailey circus with archrival James Anthony Bailey.

In her early seventies, Liz Claiborne, the fashion designer, started a foundation to fund environmental conservation projects, including projects in Brazil, Kenya, and Tibet.

At 70, Noah Webster published (in 1828) his famous New International Dictionary.

At 69, George Bernard Shaw was awarded the Nobel Prize in Literature (1925) for Back to Methuselah. *He was at work on a comedy when he died at 95.*

At 69, Ronald Reagan was the oldest person ever elected president of the United States. He served two full terms in office.

At 69, Mother Teresa won the Nobel Peace Prize and went on serving the needy until her death at age 87.

In his late sixties, Paul Cezanne painted the most powerful and valuable works of his career, masterpieces that are said to have influenced every important artist to follow.

At 67, former firefighter and gas station owner "Colonel" Harland David Sanders started the Kentucky Fried Chicken restaurant chain with a recipe he cooked up on his own.

At 66, Russian poet Boris Pasternak wrote his first novel, Dr. Zhivago.

chapter
eight

Beyond a
Reasonable Doubt

Success Story: Gil Garcetti

*There is a time for departure even when there is no
certain place to go.*
—Tennessee Williams

I f ever a sentence was the cause of a personal reinvention,
none was as shocking as this:

▶ IN THE MATTER OF THE PEOPLE of the State of California
versus Orenthal James Simpson, case number BA097211,
we the jury in the above entitled action find the defendant,
Orenthal James Simpson, *not guilty* of the crime of murder.

With that judgment, rendered inside the Los Angeles criminal
courts building at 10 a.m. on October 3, 1995, and witnessed
"live" by an estimated 150 million television viewers across America, what many called the "Trial of the Century" came to a close.

O.J. Simpson, the former NFL celebrity running back—
acquitted of fatally slashing his ex-wife Nicole and her friend,

145

Ronald Goldman—walked away a free man.

But the verdict for Simpson's chief accuser was another thing.

Widely criticized for bungling the biggest case of all, Gil Garcetti, L.A.'s district attorney and at that point America's most famous public prosecutor, found himself running the final yards of a badly damaged career.

Once a rising political star, Gil barely held onto office in the following year's election. The next time around, in the year 2000, further angered by reports that he had mismanaged a separate police corruption case, Los Angeles residents over-whelmingly voted him out.

After climbing the legal ladder for decades, at age 59, Gil Garcetti was unemployed.

"It was hurtful," he told *CBS News*. "They said, 'We've had enough. We want someone else.'"[1]

Five years later, when I met Gil, I noticed that the clenched jaw and furrowed brow that I remembered from watching him during the Simpson trial seemed to have softened over time.

But as we talked in the quiet kitchen of his Los Angeles home, I found that he could still vividly recollect the stark reality that confronted him when the salary, perks, and authority of the DA's office were suddenly wrenched from his life:

> *As a public prosecutor, I never made really large amounts of money. What am I going to do?*
>
> *I worked hard since before I was a teenager. I was always go, go, go. I gave 32 years of my life to the law, to the district attorney's office, and to the criminal justice system. I'm abso-lutely convinced that I will live in good mental and physical*

*health for another 30 years. Now I really want to do some-
thing else. But what should it be?*

During the months of his campaign for reelection, Gil had
attempted to slow down, now and then, to consider what might
happen if he lost. He gave some thought to joining a law firm or
making a run for a judgeship. But when the pressure to decide
finally hit him, the only thing he felt was confused:

*I honestly had no idea what to do. Then I got a phone call
from a man I knew. I wouldn't call him a close friend. I'd
given him some advice at one point, and he called me and
said: "You did me a favor once. Let me do you a favor now."*

*He told me: "You've never had to reinvent yourself, but I've
had to invent myself three different times, so let's talk." And
we did. And he laid it out in terms I'd never thought about before. He said, "You've known for the last 30-plus years where
you were supposed to be and what you were supposed to be
doing between 9 and 5. You're used to that structure. So why
don't you think about not being confined by that structure
anymore? If you go to work for a law firm or a corporation,
you'll be back in that structure. Why not take a little more
control of your time, Gil, and the freedom you now have?"*

*And the more I listened to him, the more sense it made.
He gave me permission to say to myself, okay, I don't need a
9-to-5 job.*

He did need something, however, and fairly soon. What
would it be? Gil never really figured that out. It appeared, quite
literally, from above.

Some seven months after his phone conversation, Gil was headed home from downtown Los Angeles after a meeting of a board on which he had volunteered to serve. As he pulled out of a parking lot and drove by a busy construction site, he looked up:

They were building the new Walt Disney Concert Hall, designed by Frank Gehry, the famous architect. The first thing I noticed was this one ironworker who was on all fours crawling across an arched steel beam at least a hundred feet off the ground. I said: Whoa! Wait a minute. I have to take a photograph of this.

I'd started carrying a camera with me in my thirties, right after my daughter was born, because you never know what you're going to see. I took some adult night school photography classes at one point. But it was more of a hobby than anything. I just always loved taking photographs.

Mesmerized by what he'd seen at the construction site, Gil returned the next morning with a better camera and a tripod:

I found this guy up in the air again. He looked like a daredevil to me, but to him he was just doing his work. And I thought: Look at the beauty, the geometry of the iron, the raw steel that's up there. But I'm way across the street, how do I get onto that site?

So I made a phone call, and at first they said no. But I eventually made a connection with some of my union friends, and they let me on. And I started taking more photographs. And over several months, I gave the ironworkers copies, and I befriended them. That's when they started insisting that I have the photos published in a book.

The ironworkers said to me: "This is going to be a world-famous building. Everybody is going to thank the architect, but nobody is going to remember us, the workers who built it."

At first, I resisted. I knew that, as a photographer, I could very easily fail. And given my high profile and what I had been through as DA, this was not going to be just a quiet failure. It was going to be very embarrassing.

But eventually Gil was persuaded, by the ironworkers and staffers at the L.A. Philharmonic, whose performances would be held in the new concert hall, that his photographs could stand on their own.

He didn't yet know it, but what had always been a hobby was about to take this nearly 60-year-old "retired" civil servant on the ride of a lifetime:

When my photo book, named Iron: Erecting the Walt Disney Concert Hall, *came out, two things happened almost immediately.*

One was that the Los Angeles Times, *the newspaper that was my nemesis when I was district attorney, all of a sudden couldn't say enough good things about me as a photographer. They were praising me to the hilt.*

The second was that, out of the blue, representatives of a major law firm contacted me and said they wanted to buy 10 or 12 of the photographs from the book. And as I'm walking into their office carrying the photographs, I stopped and said, Wait a minute: this is not a law firm full of my friends. The person who contacted me doesn't know me from Adam. They wouldn't be paying me the kind of money they're paying for

these photographs unless they think they're really worth it be-
cause law firms are notoriously cheap.
  And I realized: Maybe I really have something here.

What Gil had begun to experience was the remarkable phenomenon we've explored in previous chapters: a personal fascination and long-latent creative intelligence suddenly bursting
forth in life's second half, to form the foundation of an unpredictable new success.

Over the next several years, he upgraded his camera gear
and moved on to capture a wide range of images, from TV actors
in Hollywood to dancers in Havana.

While his shooting locations varied, a unique theme
emerged in his work—as he had with the ironworkers on the
construction site, Gil detected, in the everyday world, people and
subjects that others had missed.

Unwittingly, he was reinventing himself, marrying his new
photographic talents to the observational skills he had refined
through his previous career.

"I never thought about it that way really, but yes," Gil told
me. "As a prosecutor, I wanted to direct the system into those
areas that I felt needed exposure. Not having that authority any
longer, I started using the power of the camera."

Over time, this paid off in increasingly impressive ways.

Solo exhibitions of his work were held at UCLA's Fowler
Museum, the Millennium Art Museum in Beijing, the Virginia
Center for Architecture, the Pasadena Museum of California Art,
and the National Building Museum in Washington, D.C.

Three more books of his photographs were published; a
number of fine commercial galleries began to show and sell his
original prints.

In 2003, Gil was named one of America's four "master pho-tographers" by *American Photo Magazine*.

How could this all have possibly happened, I asked him, only a few short years after he'd been "fired"?

> *I don't know! I really can't tell you. I don't know if it was writ-ten in the stars—and this is the way it was going to be played out, and I was just a willing participant in it—or whether I can credit myself as being smart enough to see an opportu-nity and grab it. I honestly don't know. I do know that once I started taking photographs, and the ball started rolling, it was a life changing experience.*

With these changes came shifts in perspective and priorities as well. As he grew increasingly confident in his abilities and the financial pressures lessened, Gil found himself moving in a new direction: from taking pictures of things he observed to acting on them.

A New Focus

It started on a last-minute trip with his wife to rural villages in Ghana, Niger, and Mali—West African countries that are among the poorest in the world. His wife's travel was arranged by the Conrad Hilton Foundation, a philanthropy involved in health, water, and sanitation projects there.

Gil tagged along, camera gear in his backpack: "I had no end in mind," he explained. "I didn't have a specific reason for taking photographs. It was just an excuse to make the trip."

Nearly 70 percent of the people in the nations they visit-ed had no access to safe water. Millions in the region, mostly children, died from cholera, dysentery, and other water-related diseases each year.

Gil told me, "I did research, and I knew what I would find in terms of the poverty, the health problems, . . . the fact that women and young girls spent their days carrying gallons of this filthy, infested water back and forth for miles."

What he found, on arrival, impacted him even more:

What shocked me was to learn that there's actually plenty of safe water for everyone in West Africa. They're literally standing on it—it's deep underground. But these countries are incredibly poor, and they don't have the resources to get to it. I mean, it's hard to imagine.

And that's where the private foundations and nongovernmental organizations come in. They can bring in geologists and hydrologists and say, "Let's drop a well here." And when they do, they almost invariably hit safe water, and things begin to change.

First of all, health improves dramatically: people don't go blind because now they're washing with safe, clean water. The girls, five or six years old, can go to school for the first time, instead of spending their lives fetching dirty water. That was the thing that really impacted me because that's forever going to change that village, that community, that country.

Gil took photographs at every stop on his journey: mothers, infants, young girls, village gatherings, and the dry, cracked earth beneath them.

But on returning home, to the comforts of the United States, he wondered: What, if anything, can I *do* with what I have seen, and with the photos I have taken?

Then, I had an idea. And what had occurred on 9/11, the attack on the World Trade Center, brought it home for me.

I realized that the right, the moral, the ethical thing for the industrialized world to do is to help bring safe water to the people of West Africa. First, because it's there, it's the right thing to do. Secondly, you know, these are Muslim countries. We should and need to be seen as caring for Muslim people, and this is a doable, cheap thing to do.

So I went to the Hilton Foundation with my political hat on, and I said: "I'll go back as many times as I have to; you pay the expenses, and we'll produce a book together. The book will be given to nonprofits working in West Africa, and they'll be permitted to sell it to raise money for their efforts. I'll make no money myself, I'll waive my royalties, I'll sell the original photos at cost, and all the profits will go to the nonprofits."

And they bought the idea. So, then I took another three years and five trips to finish the project: interviewing people, photographing them, trying to get the story together.

Gil's large-format photograph book *Water Is Key: A Better Future for Africa* came out in late 2007.

In addition to 80 powerful images, Gil arranged to include introductory essays by former U.N. Secretary General Kofi Annan and former President Jimmy Carter, as well as short interviews with many of the West Africans he had photographed.

He explained:

The people there have an incredible beauty and inner strength about them. And this is what I wanted to show, this is what I felt was necessary. Because if you see a book of poor, desperate, dying people, how many photographs would you look at

153

before you say, "I've seen that, thank you," and then you feel guilty and walk away?

So this had to be a positive story about the resilience of these people and the fact that if you bring them safe water, their lives and the lives of generations to come in that village have been changed.

My ability to tell people about this was an important mission. I had the ability to connect through the photographs and the stories of my visits there and the ability to have people respond.

Respond they did.

The United Nations opened an exhibit of Gil's photos in the lobby of its New York headquarters. Nonprofits working in West Africa began distributing his book to raise funds.

The *Christian Science Monitor* headlined an article: "Gil Garcetti Prosecutes a New Cause—Shooting Photos That Make a Difference."[2]

Invitations for Gil to present and speak about his photos began pouring in—from colleges and universities, Rotary clubs, religious groups, men's and women's groups, and other organizations around the country.

What started as a short-term project began to expand:

My agreement with the Hilton Foundation that funded the book and the entire project was that I'd do it for a year. I'd try to raise public awareness about the issue of safe water, but I would not try to raise money.

But after about a year and a half, I realized: This is just too important, and the response is just too great. I need to do

*more. So I changed my focus: I started challenging people to
make a contribution to the organizations that actually drill
the wells in the countries I visited.*

*And what really struck me is that I touched a nerve with
every person who heard me or saw my presentation. It doesn't
make any difference whether you're a Republican or a Demo-
crat or a Libertarian, or a Tea Party member—people respond
to this.*

*Because water is such a basic need of life and the solution
is so simple.*

When I last interviewed him, Gil's photos and presentations
had helped raise enough money to drill nearly 30 wells in rural
West African villages—fountains of progress whose gifts had only
begun to surface.

Nearing age 70, he was completing a new and different project, one with a novel message of its own: the simple beauty and
wisdom of a big-city bicycle ride as a route to health, happiness,
and a cleaner environment.

At a stage of life when the vast majority of attorneys and
other professionals had long since packed it in, Gil was out mapping fresh territory for photographic success.

And in the process, he was discovering something more: the
lasting impact he could create through work that he adored.

As Gil put it:

*I was forced to reinvent myself. That sometimes happens in
life, and I'm really happy it happened to me.*

*What I learned is that you have to be receptive to new op-
portunities and ideas. And you have to be willing to fail at*

something. There's no reason now that I'd want to sit back. I'd rather try something and fail at it than just sit back and wait for something to come to me.

It's like reading the newspaper. You read the newspaper about everything that's going on in life. But what are you doing to add something to life? What are you up to? Not just in the past, but today and tomorrow?

PART THREE

Happiness
Built to Last

chapter nine

Eugeria

How Paying It Forward Pays You Back

*A human being would certainly not grow
to be 70 or 80 years old if this longevity has
no meaning for the species.*
— Carl Jung

Even before opening her doors in the heart of Montreal, the Queen Elizabeth was already the talk of North America. Built in the late 1950s by the Canadian National Railway, she was meant to be the very lap of luxury: one of the world's first grand hotels to welcome guests with air-conditioning and private telephones in each of her 1,200 splendid rooms.

Cuba's Fidel Castro was among the earliest check-ins. Queen Elizabeth herself, the Duke of Edinburgh, Princess Grace, Charles de Gaulle, and a parade of Hollywood celebrities soon followed.

And it was here, on July 16, 1962, that the crème de la crème of insurance executives, the Million Dollar Round Table of the National Association of Life Underwriters, gathered to celebrate a very profitable year.

As waiters poured coffee and the breakfast china was whisked away, Lester Rosen, the event's chairman, introduced the scheduled speaker: "The Million Dollar Round Table has invited as our guest lecturer Dr. Mortimer J. Adler, distinguished educator and author, to aid our members in their continuing search for self-development. As we share the examination of new ideas, our own lives, as well as those we touch, become richer."

The applause was exuberant: on the corporate meeting circuit, Adler was in high demand. He had taught at the University of Chicago, the University of North Carolina, and the Aspen Institute. He was host of his own weekly television show on ABC, and he had built an impressive track record coaching high-potential executives to ever-greater levels of success in their businesses and careers.

But this particular morning—as his audience contemplated their burgeoning portfolios, Adler went on the attack:

> *I do not know all the intricacies of your profession, but I am assuming that life insurance is concerned with the living as well as with the dead. Therefore, it is an aspect of life which one can insure that is the center of my consideration this morning.*[1]

Speaking during a decade when early retirement was fast becoming the national rage, Adler proceeded to liken this new American dream to digging a premature grave:

> *The retirement age is coming down from 70, to 65, to 60 and may, in the course of the next 25 years, go below that.*

But the dream come true is a nightmare.

For retirement, conceived as a protracted vacation, is a form of prolonged suicide. It marks the first formal stage on the road to oblivion.

Consider the loss to society and the deprivation of the individual involved when a man in the real prime of life, the mental, moral, and spiritual prime, is turned out to pasture at the decree of the calendar—someone who has the most creative and most socially useful part of his labor still in him.

Here is greatness wasted on the putting greens of Long Beach or the green benches of St. Petersburg.

What is the solution, or is there a solution?

Just—work. Work, not to insure your retirement, but to prevent it! You will benefit greatly from any kind of work which is a challenge to that part of you which continues growing.

It is finally time to distill wisdom from experience and to give of that wisdom.

Retire early and die early, was Adler's mantra, if not in body, then in mind and spirit. But find, instead, a way to work for the sake of others and you will step up, he asserted, "from a lower to a higher grade of life."

Who was Mortimer Adler to know or pontificate on such things? Not a clergyman or physician, Adler had a background in the field of *philosophy*.

"Exactly the point," was his frequent rejoinder, during a career that flourished for more than 70 years. "To study ancient philosophy is to know the smartest people who've ever lived."

Happily Ever After

▶ All parts of the body which have a function, if used in moderation and exercised in labors in which each is accustomed, become thereby healthy, well developed and age more slowly; but if unused and left idle, they become liable to disease, defective in growth and age quickly.

Thus prescribed Hippocrates, the father of modern medicine, in 400 BC.

But an unprecedented system for physical health was far from all that Hippocrates and his fellow Athenians invented, beginning a half millennium before Christ.

"We think and feel differently because of what a little Greek town did during a century or two" wrote classical scholar Edith Hamilton. "What was then produced . . . has never been surpassed. The Greeks came into being and the world as we know it began."[2]

Indeed, the Greeks of Athens invented the concept of democracy and, with it, the first self-government in the world. They originated deductive reasoning and the field of logic. They, quite literally, "thought up" modern mathematics and science.

Drama—both comedy and tragedy—was their creation. As were architecture and art, sculpture, music, prose, and poetry, which remain unrivaled even today.

And where the great societies before them—most notably ancient Egypt—had been preoccupied with issues of death and salvation, the Athenians were differently obsessed.

What enthralled them were matters of aliveness, and in particular the question:

What Is the Secret of Living Happily Ever After?

Out of their inquiry into this issue, these designers of western civilization invented a comprehensive approach—a philosophical system of thought and behavior—for pursuing *eugeria*, their unique term for a long and happy life.

For the Athenians, experiencing eugeria was not a matter of accumulating sufficient wealth to forevermore "kick back." Most were already men of property with bountiful supplies of leisure time.*

Unlike "simpler" animals, they reasoned, we humans are "composite creatures" who want more than to eat and sleep our lives away.

Thus, attaining genuine happiness—eugeria—requires a full-out lifelong pursuit of worthy goals through the three components of our humanity: body, mind, and soul.

This ongoing quest, they believed, was "the meaning and the purpose of life, the whole aim and end of human existence."

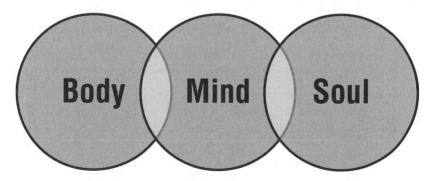

Figure 9-1. Happiness Is a Lifelong Pursuit for Body, Mind, and Soul

* Athens in the fourth and fifth centuries BC was largely a male-dominated society. For the most part, women had a limited role outside the home and were largely "kept and protected."

Let's examine the Greek's eugeria formula, one component at a time.

The Body's Pursuit: Play Hard

The fact, perhaps little known, that Plato, their greatest philosopher, was also a broad-shouldered championship wrestler says much about the way the Greeks designed their lives:

"They were the first people in the world to play," notes Edith Hamilton, "and they played on a grand scale. All over there were games; athletic contests of every description; races—horse, boat, torch races; contests in music where one side out sung the other; in dancing—on greased skins sometimes to display a nice skill of foot and balance of body; games where men leaped in and out of flying chariots, games so many that one grows weary with the list of them."[3]

And when they had worn out their bodies on the game field, they never failed to enjoy themselves in quieter ways.

"Dear to us ever," wrote Homer in his epic *Odyssey*, "is the banquet and the harp and the dance and changes of garment and the warm bath and love and sleep. A soft couch after dinner by the fire, honey-sweet wine in your glass, and nuts and beans at your elbow."

Play and pleasure were integral to the Greek life design—to their pursuit of lifelong happiness. But only up to a point. The truly happy person, they warned, must exercise *sôphrosúnê*, the virtue of self-control. Play is not an end in itself, they believed. It serves a purpose: to prepare us for the work yet to come.

Counseled Aristotle: "It would indeed be strange if one were to take trouble and suffer hardship all one's life in order to amuse oneself." But "to amuse oneself in order that one may exert oneself seems right," for "relaxation is not an end, it is taken for the sake of activity. The happy require exertion."[4]

The Mind's Pursuit: Work Hard

The Greeks were, in essence, the world's first knowledge workers. And as their unparalleled intellectual and creative achievements suggest, they never stopped exerting their minds—revisiting, refining, and rebuilding their inventions, projects, systems, and ideas:

They were the original reinventive people, the archetypes for the twenty-first-century men and women we've been visiting in this book.

For the Greeks, all things were to be questioned and explored. Knowledge work was the ultimate fun, for acquiring knowledge and experiencing enjoyment were considered one and the same. Indeed, our word school derives from *schole*, the Greek word for "leisure," which for them was the ideal opportunity for study and debate.

It was in the midst of their passionate intellectual arguments that the Greeks most experienced flow, those peak episodes of joy we examined in Chapter 3, in which one is fully absorbed by the excitement of self-chosen goals.

"The Greeks built a civilization where flow, and flow experiences, were part of everyday life," according to classicist Diane Harris-Cline. "It was a mutually supporting system that allowed the individual to find what makes them flow . . . an environment where people were allowed to excel in all areas of human achievement."[5]

Still, the Athenians realized, sporadic moments of breakthrough, however exhilarating, were not sufficient to make happiness last. To experience eugeria, to live happily ever after, there was a crucial assignment yet ahead.

The Soul's Pursuit: Pay It Forward

In his most famous work, *The Republic*, Plato argued that only by contributing the fruits of our achievements can our happiness be made everlasting.

The Greeks needed little convincing: for them, it was clear that the soulful pursuit of *paying it forward*, of working for the benefit of each other and future generations, provided the greatest payback of all:

The word *philanthropy* was derived from two Greek roots: *philo*, "love," and *anthropos*, "mankind." In the city-state of Athens, the impact of such behavior—such altruism—was evident everywhere.

The statesman Pericles is reported to have said: "We are a free democracy. We do not allow absorption in our own affairs to interfere with participation in the city's."[6]

And while there was a distinct class system in place, all Athenians were full participants in creating the "greater good." The skills of the young workers, the talents of the warriors, and the wisdom of older men were equally in high demand.

"Every Athenian as a matter of course gave time and effort to building and lifting up the common life," observed one expert historian. "They showed what miracles can be brought about when people willingly work together for the good of all."

For both the individual and society, asserted Aristotle, miracles become commonplace, when the soul is engaged: "There is a life which is higher than the measure of humanity; to live according to the highest thing that is in a man, for small though it be, in power and worth it is far above the rest."

The Eugeria Paradigm

The lifelong pursuit of excellence (*arête*), with the goal of contributing our accomplishments to others—this, to the Greeks, was the ultimate formula, the blueprint, for eugeria, a long and happy life:

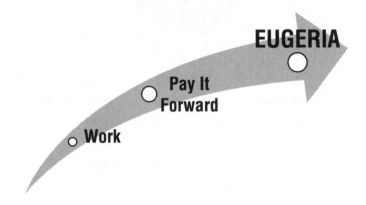

But is there any evidence that they had it right?

In separate, unprecedented studies, in 1994 and 2007, researchers at the Royal Society of Medicine in London, as well as on the ground in Greece, explored this very question.

And they reached the same, previously unrecognized, yet remarkable bottom line.

Using all available sources of historical information, investigators set out to identify men of intellectual excellence and achievement who lived in the fifth and fourth centuries BC—in other words, the very Greeks whose philosophy and lifestyle we've been discussing.

To ensure the purity of their sample, they included men who died of natural causes as well as those known to have died violently (by execution, murder, poisoning, suicide, or disease).

The result was a cohort of 83 influential Greeks whose dates of birth and death could be precisely verified.

And according to the researchers, this is what the data showed:

▶ CONTRARY TO THE COMMONLY held belief that in antiquity and as late as 1700 A.D. normal lifespan was about 35 years, many men of fame are known to have lived longer lives characterized by eugeria, happy aging. *Their mean and median lengths of life were found to be 71.3 and 70 years, respectively, equal to that of the civilized populations of modern times.*[7]

Among those identified by the examiners were three centenarians: the astronomer Aristarchus, the natural philosopher Democritus, and the rhetorician Gorgias, who died at the age of 108, in 275 BC.

As well, it had previously been known that Plato's rival Isocrates lived to 98, the great tragedian Sophocles lived to 90, and Plato himself lived to 80; further, all had continued to work and contribute prolifically, well into what is still today considered a very ripe old age.

In other words:

The new studies showed that, rather than the exception, living a long, happy life was commonplace in ancient Greece.

How could this be explained?

In seeking answers, researchers noted that genetics and living conditions may have played a role: the climate was mild; nutrition, housing, and sanitary conditions were generally good; and slaves were available to handle heavyweight chores.

But basics such as these, according to the lead scientist, Dr. Menelaos Batrinos, professor of endocrinology at Athens University Medical School, missed the central point.

It was the Athenians' *philosophy*, their design for living, that may have mattered most, he concluded in his final report:

▶ OF THE GREATEST IMPORT was an intense intellectual and animated social life in which the aged actively participated . . . and, not least of all, the respect that they were accorded for their ongoing role and contribution. Thus ancient Greece provided not only new scientific and very advanced ideas for their time, but also a good paradigm of eugeria and eulongevity.

The Echo of Greece

While the Athenian paradigm has faded into history, the thinking behind it has endured through the ages — most especially its soulful tenet: that *paying it forward*, working for the sake of others, pays us back in unexpected ways.

This message resounds from the Old Testament:

▶ DO NOT BE HARDHEARTED or tightfisted toward your poor brother. Give generously to him and do so without a grudging heart; then because of this the Lord your God will bless you in all your work and everything you put your hand to.
—*Deuteronomy 15:7–8*

To the New Testament:

▶ GIVE AND IT WILL BE GIVEN to you. A good measure pressed down, shaken together and running over, will be poured into your lap. For with the measure you use, it will be measured to you.

—*Luke 6:38*

From an American transcendentalist:

▶ IT IS ONE OF THE MOST beautiful compensations of this life that no man can sincerely help another without helping himself.

—*Ralph Waldo Emerson*

To a German-born physicist:

▶ WE ARE HERE FOR THE SAKE of others. Many times a day, I realize how much my outer and inner life is built upon the labors of people, both living and dead, and how earnestly I must exert myself in order to give in return as much as I have received.

—*Albert Einstein*

To a Buddhist head of state:

▶ I HAVE FOUND THAT the more we care for the happiness of others, the greater is our own sense of well-being. Cultivating a close, warmhearted feeling for others is the principal source of success in life.

—*Tenzin Gyatso, the fourteenth Dalai Lama of Tibet*

Over the past century, experts in a variety of disciplines have increasingly sought to assess the validity of such statements through the tools of modern science and analysis.

Early among them was Sigmund Freud, who is often quoted as asserting that loving others and expressing ourselves through our work pay us back with the benefits of mental health.

Freud didn't personally examine the dynamics of this phenomenon beyond the early stages of the human life cycle, but an up-and-coming pioneer, trained in part by Freud's daughter Anna, went on to do just that.

He was Erik Erikson, a name that became synonymous with a post-Freudian breakthrough that forever altered psychology's view of human development.

In the 1950s, Erikson put forth a comprehensive life model, uncannily similar to ancient Greek wisdom, in which love and work were seen as fundamental to a life of happiness and well-being "at the beginning, in the middle, or at the end."[8]

Acknowledging the ancient roots of his thinking, Erickson, who became a Harvard professor and Pulitzer Prize winner wrote: "Each generation must find the wisdom of the ages in the form of its own wisdom."

His model outlined a sequence of developmental stages and the accompanying challenges that we must meet, over the course of our lives, in order to avoid stagnation and thrive:

Challenge 1

"In youth, you must find out what you care to do and who you care to be."

Challenge 2

"In young adulthood you learn whom you care to be with, at work and in private life."

Challenge 3

"In adulthood you learn to know what and whom you can take care of."

Erikson, who originated the notion of "identity crisis," labeled the third level of challenge—which grows exponentially more important after midlife—the task of *generativity*, his personal term for *paying it forward*.

▶ ADULT MAN IS SO CONSTITUTED as to *need to be needed* lest he suffer the mental deformation of self-absorption. . . . He requires the challenge emanating from what he has generated. I refer to *man's love for his works and ideas as well as for his children*. Generativity, as the instinctual power behind various forms of selfless "caring," potentially extends to whatever a man generates and leaves behind, creates and produces or hopes to produce.[9]

Put most succinctly, he said, "I am what survives me."

And, as did the Greek masters before him, Erickson held firmly to the conviction that by creating a legacy through our love and work, by paying it forward, we generate, for ourselves, a higher order of existence—a level of well-being and self-fulfillment that is otherwise rarely experienced.

Miraculous Recovery

Late on the afternoon of December 31, 2005, a 97-year-old man was at home in Houston when a sharp pain ripped through his upper chest and between his shoulder blades, then moved into his neck.

"It never occurred to me to call 911 or my physician," he later recalled. "You are, in a sense, a prisoner of the pain, which was intolerable. You're thinking, what could I do to relieve myself of it? If it becomes intense enough, you're perfectly willing to accept cardiac arrest as a possible way to get rid of the pain."[10]

But instead, his heart kept beating; and after initially refusing hospitalization, five weeks later he became the oldest person in history to survive an operation to repair a torn aorta, the main artery leading from the heart.

A number of top physicians at Methodist Hospital and Baylor College of Medicine expected him to die during surgery or shortly thereafter, and, unquestionably, his recovery was touch and go.

The patient was on a ventilator for six weeks, unable to breath on his own. He needed dialysis because of kidney failure. He spent a month in a windowless intensive care unit, at times delirious and unresponsive, with doctors concerned that he'd suffered irreversible brain damage.

Then, on Sunday, April 2, the hospital's lung specialist, Dr. William Lunn, brought his own 8-year-old daughter, Elizabeth, to work with him, telling her that one of his patients was doing poorly. Elizabeth drew a cheerful picture of a rainbow, butterflies, trees, and grass and asked her father to present it to his patient.

"You should have seen his eyes brighten," Dr. Lunn said. The patient soon asked to see young Elizabeth, and he held her hand and thanked her. Over the next six months, he recovered fully enough to be back working nearly a full day. "I feel very good," he said. "I'm getting back into the swing of things."

As unprecedented as this case was, even more remarkable was the fact that the patient was the very man who, more than 50 years earlier, had pioneered the heart surgery that saved his life; *and* the first successful coronary bypass operation; *and* the first surgery to transplant four organs—a heart, two kidneys, and a lung—from one donor to different recipients; and the list goes on.

Indeed, the patient was Dr. Michael E. DeBakey, sought out by kings, presidents, celebrities, and heart patients worldwide as the greatest cardiovascular surgeon of all time.

In total, DeBakey performed some 60,000 surgeries up until age 90, when he shifted his attention "because there were so many other things that needed to be done," he said, including patient evaluations, postoperative care, long-term follow-up studies, and laboratory research on a new cardiac assistive device.[11]

It was during this final phase of DeBakey's 70-plus-year medical career—in fact just months before his own medical emergency—that DeBakey received a letter from Dr. Shep Nuland, the Connecticut-based surgeon turned award-winning author whom we met in Chapter 2 of this book.

Shep, at age 75, was planning to write a book on the secrets of successful aging and longevity, and asked to visit with DeBakey, who was age 96 at the time.

Within a few weeks, Shep was warmly received in Houston by DeBakey and his second wife, Katrina, who was younger than DeBakey by some four decades.

"It was fascinating," Shep recalled:

*I got to know him in those two days when we were together,
and he talked constantly about himself, which was just what
I wanted, because I think I got the answers. Part of it had to
do with the exquisite egotism of Mike DeBakey, who wanted
you to know what his secrets were. I would say to him, "You
know, you're this amazing fellow," and essentially, without
putting it in words, he said, "Yes, I am this amazing fellow
and here's why."*

In their conversations, DeBakey told Shep that his continuing work, well into his life's tenth decade, was motivated
by a sense of insatiable curiosity—a drive to keep learning new
things—and that this was a wellspring of his longevity.

But feeling instinctively that there was "something else" to
DeBakey's "astounding vitality," Shep kept probing, at one point
taking Katrina DeBakey aside at the end of a dinner party:

*She said it was love. He was working very, very hard because
there's somebody it's focused on. It's focused on that man or
woman in the bed who comes to DeBakey because he's the
final answer. If he can't give it to them, nobody can. So it's
not work in the abstract—it's love, very much directed toward
individual human beings.*

At first, Shep was surprised by this because DeBakey was
notorious for being tough and abrupt with his medical residents
and colleagues. But with his patients, Shep discovered, things
were different:

*I gradually came to see, both from his direct statements and
by listening for it between the lines when he was discussing*

his longevity, that beyond all else, the factor that had given meaning to this unexpectedly sensitive man's career was his ability to bring hope to the tens of thousands of individual men and women for whom he had cared. As he told me, "The gratification comes from the feeling that you've done something important for people."

In the book he later wrote, *The Art of Aging*, Shep, the 75-year-old surgeon, concluded this from his study of DeBakey, the elder surgeon:

The dividends of such a life can come to each of us, in an awareness of having contributed something of value. It is in the very real sense a bountiful gift, one that must surely manifest itself not only in emotional but physiological ways, as well.[12]

As if to underscore Shep's observations, DeBakey maintained an active work schedule for more than a year following what doctors—many of them his former students—termed his "miraculous recovery" from heart surgery. He passed away just two months short of his one hundredth birthday.

Molecules of Compassion

Can we extrapolate a viable strategy for ourselves from Michael DeBakey's example?

What about from the ancient Athenians who, in their energetic pursuit of a long, happy life, lived twice the average lifespan, thousands of years ago?

Was Erik Erikson on target when he claimed that generativity—paying it forward through loving and working for the sake of others—pays us back powerfully in life's second half?

Is this universally so?

Interest in issues such as these, once primarily the domain of philosophers and theologians, has spread in recent years through the halls of academia, medicine, social science, public health, and even business and economics, generating hundreds of fresh, related uncertainties and millions of dollars in research funds.

At the top of the pile of questions is one that overarches all others and has been elevated, of late, into a global evolutionary debate:

Were We Born to Be Generous?

Or to phrase it more scientifically: Is it naturally to our advantage to love and care for others? Are we organically rewarded when we act altruistically because we were meant, or have evolved, to be this way?

Nature offers numerous examples of paying it forward, of creatures acting altruistically at their own expense. Bees lay down their lives to defend the hive. Certain monkeys, prairie dogs, chickens, and songbirds sound the alarm at an approaching predator, risking their own safety by drawing attention to themselves.

But for people to behave this way would seem a violation of evolutionary doctrine. For in the human world, the canon of natural selection—survival of the fittest and the genes of the fittest—is said to rule. Wrote Darwin in the *Descent of Man*, "He who was ready to sacrifice his life, as many a savage has been, rather than betray his comrades, would often leave no offspring to inherit his noble nature."[13]

If evolutionary fitness is necessarily selfish, how could it possibly explain altruism? How could it allow, let alone encourage us, to take care of others—if we end up worse off?

Darwin puzzled over this and ultimately concluded: perhaps we don't.

In an evolution of his own thinking, he realized that seemingly self-sacrificial behavior, though potentially disadvantageous to the individual, might be beneficial at the group level: "A tribe including many members who . . . were always ready to give aid to each other and sacrifice themselves for the common good, would be victorious over most other tribes; and this would be natural selection."

In the past several decades, experts on the leading edge of evolutionary biology, neuroscience, and psychology have stepped into this discussion, giving birth to a wide range of explanations as to why empathy, cooperation, altruism, and evolution might naturally go hand in hand.

At the University of Virginia, for example, Professor Jonathan Haidt has hypothesized that, in the scheme of evolution, human beings "are the giraffes of altruism." That is, in the same way that giraffes developed long necks to survive, people have grown moral minds to enable them to adapt to and flourish in their environment.[14]

It would take many pages to analyze the full range of emerging arguments and theories on this topic. And it is well beyond the scope of this book to adequately catalogue them.

Suffice it to say, however, that it is increasingly difficult to dismiss the mounting body of evidence—compelling though perhaps not scientifically conclusive—that within the human organism there are mechanisms that, as a matter of course, produce happiness and longevity as outcomes of generosity and altruistic behavior.

The Warm Glow of Giving

Harvard Business School might be the last place you would expect to find first-of-a-kind research on the emotional benefits of *giving money away.*

But in 2010, a team led by Harvard marketing professor Michael I. Norton released an international study of people in 136 countries that observed the following:

▶ CAN MONEY BUY HAPPINESS? Apparently it can—if that money is spent on someone else. In contrast to traditional economic thought, which places self-interest as the guiding principle of human motivation, our findings suggest that the reward experienced from helping others may be deeply ingrained in human nature, emerging in diverse cultural and economic contexts.[15]

The Harvard team focused on "prosocial spending," conducting surveys that asked people to reflect on times when they used their financial resources to help others. Of particular interest was whether people living in very poor countries, and thus concerned with satisfying their own basic needs, would feel differently from those surveyed in wealthy nations.

They did not: "Across countries and through various income levels, researchers found that subjects who spend more money on gifts and charitable donations described themselves as happier."

The study concluded: "Although spending money on others differed in both form and frequency in poor versus rich countries, the emotional benefits were consistent. *Much like eating or sex, generosity seems to generate positive feelings in almost everyone, regardless of cultural context.*"

Without elaborating, the Harvard team noted that the feelings reported were consistent with a term often utilized by behavioral economists: the *warm glow effect*.

For decades, without necessarily delving into its physiological origins, economists have defined this phenomenon as follows:

▶ A WARM GLOW EFFECT is the enjoyment derived by contributors to charities or other good works when they consider the benefits realized by the beneficiaries.[16]

What does this sensation of enjoyment mean? And where does it come from?

Multiple experiments in recent years appear to hold the answer. Among them are brain scans conducted by neuroscientists at the National Institutes of Health and the Center for Cognitive Neurosciences at the University of Oregon, where psychology Professor Ulrich Mayr teamed up with a group of economists to localize and measure the "warm glow" of charitable giving. Mayr explained:

▶ FOR OBVIOUS REASONS, you can't simply ask people, "Do you give money because you want to make a good impression or because you really care?"

So we needed first to find a way to get at people's deepest motives. And one way to do that is to look at the brain areas that determine what motivates us. And these are evolutionary ancient areas in the middle of the brain; the most prominent one is called the *nucleus accumbens*; they respond to basic pleasures such as food, social comfort, sweets. If these pleasure areas respond to improvements in the well-being of others, then this would provide a direct measure of pure altruism.[17]

Each of the participants in the experiments was given $100 and then asked to crawl into a magnetic resonance imaging (MRI) scanner for an hourlong session in which they viewed financial transactions on a computer screen. They were told that they could keep whatever money remained at the end of the session.

"They then saw a series of scenarios," Mayr reported, "in which a certain amount of money was taken out of their pocket and a certain amount was given to a charity's account. As a charity, we used the local food bank. We did find that money going to the charity from your own account actually elicits neural activity in those very pleasure areas that we talked about."

Said William T. Harbaugh, a member of the National Bureau of Economic Research, "To economists, the surprising thing . . . is that we actually see people getting rewards as they give up money. Neural firing in this fundamental, primitive part of the brain is larger when your money goes to a nonprofit charity to help other people."[18]

The Helper's High

Related, but distinct, physiological effects have been documented in numerous studies of people who volunteer their time and efforts for the benefit of others.

What's commonly referred to as *helper's high* — a sense of euphoria and energy, followed by a longer period of calm — is not a figment of our imagination, experts say.

Whether it is the *cause* of generous behavior, the effect, or both, however, has yet to be fully determined. Human emotions and related behaviors are complex clusters of chemical and neural responses. And while much has been learned about the neurobiology of stress and aggression, the science that underlies compassion is relatively unexplored territory.

The experience of helper's high was once thought to be connected to the release of pleasure-linked chemicals, such as dopamine and endorphins, in the brain.

More recently, however, there has been considerable focus on the hormone oxytocin.

Well known for its role in preparing pregnant women, physically and emotionally, for childbirth and motherhood, oxytocin levels appear to increase, and stress levels decrease, when we are engaged in other forms of self-sacrifice and helping behavior.[19]

In fact, because of its apparent links to a wide range of emotion-laden activities—ranging from orgasm to pair bonding and social recognition, as well as volunteering—scientists increasingly call it the "love hormone."

The Fabric of Longevity

Early in 2011, Richard P. Sloan, a professor of behavioral medicine at the Columbia University Medical Center, wrote an opinion column in the *New York Times* that asserted, in part, the following:

▶ THERE'S NO EVIDENCE to back up the idea that an upbeat attitude can prevent any illness or help someone recover from one more readily. Cancer doesn't care if we're good or bad, virtuous or vicious, compassionate or inconsiderate. Neither does heart disease or AIDS or any other illness or injury.[20]

In so stating, Sloan revisited a question that has a lengthy history in American cultural discourse: Does our attitude or behavior have any genuine power over health or longevity?

Among those who immediately responded to Sloan's comments was Stephanie L. Brown, a medical research scientist at the Department of Veterans Affairs (VA) and the University of Michigan who had been studying the benefits of generativity—paying it forward—for years.

Wrote Brown:

▶ ALTHOUGH WE ENDORSE his skepticism regarding scientific evidence for the power of positive thinking, it is critical to qualify his point. Our work, and that of others, has demonstrated that helping behavior and compassionate motives are associated with reduced morbidity and mortality for the helper. We must not let misinterpretation and misrepresentation of some scientific findings obscure others.[21]

Indeed, well-regarded health and longevity studies on individuals who care for others during the second half of their own lives have been under way for decades, in a range of settings and situations:

• A pioneering 15-year study of a particular order of American nuns, the School Sisters of Notre Dame, was initially intended by the National Institute on Aging to answer questions about who gets Alzheimer's disease and why. The 678 sisters involved were considered ideal for scientific study because they shared a stable, similar lifestyle over the years—same diet, little drinking, no smoking, never pregnant, most were teachers in Catholic schools—thus limiting variables that can skew human research results.

A team led by David A. Snowdon, an epidemiologist at the University of Kentucky, ended up with more than it set out to. Its findings, reported in 2001, not only documented resistance to Alzheimer's among the nuns but showed significantly increased longevity, compared to other women. In one convent alone, there were seven centenarians, many of them free from dementia.

"You don't necessarily have to join a church or join a convent," Dr. Snowdon said. "But that love of other people, that caring, how good they are to each other and patient, that's something all of us can do."[22]

- In 2004, researchers at the Johns Hopkins University Medical Centers reported the results of a randomized experiment in which 128 people, ages 60 to 86, were split into two groups. Half spent 15 hours per week as reading tutors for Baltimore elementary school kids. The other half didn't work, serving as a control group. During follow-up, it was found that "physical, cognitive, and social activity" and body strength increased significantly for those who served as tutors, while decreasing for those who did not. Each of these factors, according to the researchers, "is an independent predictor of important health outcomes in late life."[23]

- At Stanford University in 2005, Professor Emeritus Carl Thoresen released the results of a national study of more than 7,500 Americans aged 70 and older. The purpose of his research was to test the hypothesis that people in this age group who volunteer frequently tend to live longer in general. The findings? Indeed, they do. This was especially

so among people who otherwise had limited social inter-
action. The Stanford data reaffirmed the discoveries of
numerous other studies, including those undertaken at the
University of California–Berkeley, the University of Michigan, and the University of Texas, where Professor Marc
Musick summarized his findings this way: "Simply adding
the volunteering role was protective of mortality."[24]

Could the similar results in these studies be matters of coin-
cidence? Yes, certainly it's possible.

There are some who contend that, like research linking exercise with happiness and longevity, the kind of data I've cited
is scientifically inconclusive. It's correlative, they say—meaning
that while there may be some connection between love, work for
the sake of others, and living a happy, longer life, it's not something you can prove or rely on.

They argue: Perhaps people who choose to pay it forward
are naturally happier to begin with. Maybe genetics determines
our lifespan no matter what. You can't ignore the fact that caring
for others too much may lead to burnout and health problems for
the caretaker.

The naysayers could be right—generativity may not be a
one-size-fits-all prescription.

But, like the ancient Greeks, the reinventive people I met
while writing this book took it as an article of faith, a slam dunk,
that whatever achievements they might attain in life's second
half ought not to be kept to themselves.

Rejecting the common lockstep of life and repudiating the
notion of ever retiring, each turned an inner fascination into a
new form of work, into self-created challenges that they loved, that

allowed them to develop their full potential, and in many cases, that generated a significant income. Moreover, they found a way to leverage their new work, to transform it into a gift to the future.

Reinventing their personal success, each designed a life and legacy that mattered to others.

As we've seen in previous chapters, *Gil Garcetti*, the former district attorney, did this through his photography. *Marion Rosen*, trained as a physical therapist, accomplished it through her teaching and entrepreneurship. *Shep Nuland*, the "retired" surgeon, did it through his writing. *Horace Deets*, the former head of AARP, achieved it through his mentoring and consulting.

In the pages to come, we'll explore how career psychologist *Rita K. Spina*, nurse midwife *Sharon Rising*, and former marketing executive *Mark Goldsmith* accomplished this in still other ways.

In my visits with all of them, what I encountered were vibrant individuals who never quit—who continued to love, succeed, and flourish in their lives and work, well into their seventies, eighties, even nineties.

And in the process, to hear them tell it, they unwrapped the rewards of a heartfelt philosophy that has echoed through the ages:

▶ THIS IS THE ONE TRUE JOY in life, the being used for a purpose recognized by yourself as a mighty one; the being a force of nature instead of a feverish, selfish little clod of ailments and grievances, complaining that the world will not devote itself to making you happy.

I am of the opinion that my life belongs to the whole community and as long as I live it is my privilege to do for it whatever I can. I want to be thoroughly used up when I die, for the harder I work, the more I live.

Life is no "brief candle" to me.

It is a sort of splendid torch which I have got hold of for the moment, and I want to make it burn as brightly as possible before handing it on to future generations.

— George Bernard Shaw, Irish playwright, activist, Nobel laureate, and Oscar winner who continued working until his death at age 94

chapter ten

The Road to Reinvention

Success Story: Rita K. Spina

Do not go where the path may lead, go instead where there is no path and leave a trail.
— Ralph Waldo Emerson

She was always ahead of the curve.

Long before unhappy suburban housewives started divorcing their husbands, Rita K. Spina did just that. Years before single moms commonly headed households, Rita raised four children on her own.

Decades before many women attended college, she earned a BA, an MA, and a PhD. And way before the male-dominated New York psychology world had seen anything like her, Rita launched a long, successful career as a clinical practitioner and expert in the field.

"I know I'm a risk taker," she explained. "I've always needed to do things that nobody else would do, say things that nobody else would say."

I first came to know Rita when I was teaching at the graduate business school at the University of North Carolina at Chapel Hill. My wife, Jane, came home from a local meeting one day with a look of astonishment and said: "There's this woman you absolutely have to meet. She says she's 70 years old, but it's hard to believe. When I'm that age, that's how I want to be."

Jane and I met Rita a few weeks later at an Italian restaurant on Franklin Street, the main thoroughfare adjacent to the Carolina campus. As usual on a weekday evening, the bar and tables were filled with professors and working professionals, ranging from their mid-thirties to late forties, our age bracket at the time.

When Rita walked in, I barely looked up—I figured she was just one more regular customer. But when Jane introduced us and Rita settled in across from me, I couldn't help but sit and stare.

Born in 1927, this woman was my mother's age, but she seemed hardly of the same generation. From the clothes she wore to the way she thought, expressed, and carried herself, it was as if the difficult experiences she had lived through, the challenges she'd tackled, had infused her with youthful electricity, rather than taking it away.

One thing I learned about Rita early on: she rarely spent time looking back.

So it took some doing to pin her down—more than a decade later—when I returned to North Carolina, from my new home in California, for the purpose of chronicling Rita's story for this book.

Sitting on a screened porch behind her contemporary home, several days before her eightieth birthday, Rita appeared exactly the same as when we first met: "80 is just a number attached to me," she said. "I have no timeline. I'm no different than I've ever been."

That hit the nail on the head: through all of Rita's life, she'd sought new and different ways to reinvent herself.

She told me:

For as long as I can remember, I always needed to be excellent at something. That's what drove me to be a mother, I had to perform. But after I had my children, I couldn't just stay home. I mean, in the 1950s, who the hell was a woman who got a divorce with four children and raised them herself?

I'm not saying it was easy—it was very difficult—but I found out I could do it. And I felt I did a relatively good job. And that, I think, released me, because once I had this family, I became very brave. I needed to do something more, take another risk. I was the only woman I knew who was like that. And, in many ways, I still am.

It's not as though she didn't try to live more normally—now and then.

In her early forties, while one of America's first female corporate psychologists, Rita met Larry Spina, a successful small business owner, at a dinner party hosted by friends.

They were married in a matter of months—and this time around, it worked:

It was so different from my first marriage; there was such a connection. We could say anything to one another. To take on a woman and four children was a huge risk. But he was always so sure of himself. And he was always right. He was a very smart guy, and he had a great sense of humor. He was what I needed in my life.

Over the next decade, while she worked *and* earned her doctoral degree, Larry helped to raise Rita's children—Susan, David, Beth, and Nancy—and send them off to college.

When she headed up the Department of Psychology at the Kings Park School District, on the north shore of Long Island, Larry had dinner waiting for her at night.

And when, in her mid-fifties, Rita moved to Hofstra University, as the director of the Psychological Evaluation and Research Center, and taught, and ran her own private practice, Larry was there to back her up.

By the time they reached their sixties, Larry, who was four years older, was burned out.

On vacation in North Carolina, they fell in love with the rolling hills of Chatham County.

Once home to a thriving dairy industry, the area was now dotted with small sustainable farms backing up to cozy hamlets that were peopled by young families, vacation home owners, and retirees.

Larry was ready to join them.

But a few months after moving there, Rita was bored silly:

I hated to leave New York, but Larry wanted to retire earlier than I did. He started playing tennis every day. I played a lot of tennis at first too. I made friends, and there were book clubs, and I would join them, but they were never enough. I couldn't just hang out.

For me, it began somewhat unconsciously. I didn't want to finish my life that way, doing nothing other than relaxing. I was looking at people my age and older and saying: I don't want to be like that. I wanted to accomplish something, do something to continue developing myself. That's the way I'd always been.

But rather than a developmental period, what lay ahead for Rita was a painful demolition project. For new growth to occur, her previous ground of being had to be cleared.

Severing a Former Identity

Over the next few years, Rita tried to circle back, professionally. Still thinking of herself as a psychologist, she looked for ways to continue working in the field. "I was in a totally different milieu, but my head was still where I'd been for years and years."

She took a series of part-time assignments: teaching psychology to health-care workers at a Durham, North Carolina, technical school and training nurse candidates on people skills at a local hospital. But for this now 63-year-old master of her craft, jobs such as these proved tedious and unfulfilling.

Soon, things went from dull to absurd. In Raleigh, the capital, Rita was told she had to take North Carolina's licensing exam in order to practice psychology in her new home state. It was the same test she'd passed decades earlier in New York, when she first began her career:

> *It made me so angry. Here I'd done all this work, and they wanted me to take this test all over again. But I was going to show them! So I started looking up all this stuff and studying it. And one day Larry came home and said: "Why are you cramming like this? It's making you miserable. You're not even there in your head anymore."*

And the psychologist in me realized he was right. I was stuck in my old identity. What I really needed was to tear away from it. And that night I closed my old psychology files and books and stuck them in a big box in the attic, and that was the end of it. It was quite a big deal for me at the time.

In fact, the big deal was yet to come.

The Route to Reinvention

Her energy depleted and plans uncertain, Rita flew out to Oregon where, ironically, her middle daughter, Beth, was completing her own PhD in psychology.

On an unusually clear day, they headed from Portland toward the coast, following Highway 26, the route that parallels and, in places, runs directly atop the path that formed the original Oregon Trail.

As they traversed the rolling hills of the Tillamook and Clatsop state rainforests—once so dense with giant evergreens that Lewis and Clark were forced to end their expedition there—for Rita, a new journey began:

I saw the denuding of the mountains, the clear-cutting of the trees for logging, and I was horrified. I remember crying, I was so upset by it. I couldn't believe that people just came in and cleared this out with no respect for what was happening to the beauty of the world around us.

For mile after mile, the old growth forest had been stripped away. In the emptiness that echoed inside her, though she did not yet know it, Rita had found the road to reinvention.

Returning home, she developed a curious new habit: gathering oddly shaped pieces of wood and storing them in her garage. What for? I asked her.

I was just fooling around with it. I loved wood. I liked the way it felt. And living where we were in Chatham County, which was filled with forest, it was all around.

But what was she going to do with it?

I had no idea where I was going, no thoughts in my mind. As far as I was concerned, I was still a psychologist. Whether or not I realized I was in transition, I'm not sure.

That Rita's life was changing, radically, soon became unmistakably clear.

She received a phone call: while on the tennis court, Larry had died of a sudden heart attack. At that point, they had been married and best friends for nearly 25 years:

The fact that we had found each other helped me to become who I was because I could always weigh things with him. When we moved to North Carolina, I had moved further away from every piece of my life. Now, when Larry died, I was totally on my own. And I went through a really tough time because he had set the foundation, you know, between the two of us, the foundation that we were going to live on.

After he was gone, there was no guideline for me—he wasn't coming home.

Finding Flow

Following Larry's death, Rita would often awaken at three-thirty or four in the morning. Rather than tossing and turning, or trying to read, she would make a cup of coffee and go upstairs to a tiny studio that she'd created on the second floor of their home.

"Comfort, release, therapy," she said, was all she was after. "Trying to do something with my hands and not think about the painful things."

But it was in the silent darkness of these hours that a strange new glimmer of joy—a sense of flow—enveloped her.

It was here that the person Rita would next become, first started to appear:

> *Somehow or another it was all related to what I had seen and experienced on my trip to Oregon. That was the beginning of my new work. Along with collecting wood, I had begun to go to junkyards and find things that were man-made—in other words, pieces of metal and technological kinds of things. And I began to put these together in three-dimensional pieces and have ideas about how these elements played off of one another.*
>
> *Which was going to win? Was it the world and its natural self, or the technological world, which was getting bigger and more important? Or was it possible for them to somehow work together?*
>
> *As a psychologist, I'd always put people and ideas together. Now, I was putting things and ideas together. And that fit me very well. Was my art any good? Would the message ever get out there? That, I didn't know.*

Only vaguely aware of it before, Rita would discover that Chatham County was fast becoming a breeding ground for artists and artisans, as former mills and factories in towns like Pittsboro, the county seat, were renovated into restaurants, craft shops, and galleries that drew both locals and tourists.

Soon enough, she met a group of eight women artists, including several highly successful professionals: a fiber artist, a painter, and a sculptor among them. Though older in years than most, Rita was, artistically speaking, "the baby" in the group. In fact, she hardly believed that what she was making in her studio could be considered art at all.

Her new mentors put the kibosh on that thinking: "Don't let anybody tell you what you're doing doesn't have any meaning," they would say. "If it has meaning for you, that's what's important."

Structuring the Future

One brisk winter afternoon, not long after she first began fiddling with metal and wood, Rita carried several of her three-dimensional creations into a large reception room at Fearrington Village, a local complex that included homes, quaint shops, and a country inn.

Despite her protests that she wasn't good enough, Rita's artist friends had convinced her to display her work, side-by-side with theirs, in an exhibition and sale:

I kept arguing, and they said "No, you have to be part of it." I had to work to get the stuff finished, to get it there, and it was my first trial, in a sense. I was nervous, very unsure of myself. What was I doing here? And lo and behold, I sold my first piece of art. I was shocked—not so much that I had created it but that somebody wanted it enough to pay for it.

And for a long while after, when my art started selling more widely, and I was invited to exhibit my work around the state, it was hard for me to accept when people asked me: "How did you come to create this?" Because there's a certain transformation that occurs when you shift from being the person you always were—in my case a psychologist—to something new.

My art was becoming the core of me now.

That assessment, however, would prove premature, for there was a further transformation yet to come.

Payback Time

Some 15 years after she moved to semirural North Carolina, Rita sat up with neighbors as the anchorman on WRAL-TV, the local CBS station, began his 11 p.m. report: "Years of debate ended tonight when Chatham County Commissioners voted 4 to 1 to approve plans for Briar Chapel, the largest mixed-use development the county has ever seen."

"Bye-bye," wrote the area newspaper, "to 1,600 acres of mostly undisturbed woodlands and pastures. Hello to 6,000 new neighbors buying 2,400 new homes at up to $1 million each, and to three new commercial centers."

They couldn't have been more wrong—for it was in the battle over Briar Chapel that Rita's reinvention hit full stride:

All of a sudden, in this beautiful forested area in which I lived, the developers were coming in. It was like my Oregon experience all over again—they were going to come in behind me and strip the land. And because we all knew each other living in this area, and there were 26 homes, including mine, directly confronted by this issue, a few of us got together. It was then that, along with the other things I was doing, I became a civic activist as well.

I was 76 years old when it started. I had my art, which had replenished me emotionally and earned me a little money. Now I wanted to give something back. In a sense, it was pay-back time.

With three other homeowners, Rita organized a grassroots action and lobbying organization, the Chatham Citizens for Effective Communities, whose message echoed that of her artwork: with thoughtful planning, both the natural environment and human progress can coexist, side-by-side.

At county planning sessions, she stood and warned the commissioners: "With the density of growth to come in the next 10 years, it is incumbent upon you to provide us with assurances that the beauty of this county can be preserved."

When they did not offer such guarantees, Rita's group, through its rapidly expanding membership, voted to replace them with politicians who did. "I was always polite," she told me, "but I've always had a big mouth when necessary."

And she hardly quit her jawboning there.

At age 77, Rita worked to design and launch a second salvo against uncontrolled growth: the first-of-a-kind Citizens College—its curriculum designed to bring county officials and residents into the classroom together, and into a dialogue about the types of development that could benefit everyone involved.

"The goal of the college is to raise your awareness that you have as much responsibility as the people who are in power working for you," Rita told students—who ranged from doctors and lawyers to stay-at-home moms—"and you have to learn how to deal with that."

Learn and deal they did. By the end of its fourth year, the college had sent nearly 100 graduates back into the community, and it had helped to position many of them on county advisory boards, in homeowners' associations, and in other key spots where they could positively influence change.

Said Rita of such accomplishments: "We've been very effective."

Body, Mind, and Soul

As we reached the end of our visit, this nearly 80-year-old woman literally sprung from her chair—slightly late for a seminar she was scheduled to lead.

I stayed behind for a few moments, gathering my thoughts and notes and watching as the summer sun dropped into the top of the woods—into the crown of the thick pine forest that was still there, behind Rita's house.

No one had come to cut it down.

Scattered around her yard were examples of her outdoor artwork: large, elegant flowers made of scrap metal, discarded tree trunks carved into shapes that seemed to have a life of their own.

Driving north on Highway 15-501, back toward Chapel Hill, I observed that the road, while recently widened, still had a countrylike feel. Yes, there were a few fresh shopping clusters here and there, but no giant strip malls had appeared.

And where Briar Chapel, the feared "mother of all suburban sprawl" was to have been, stood an attractive stone entryway to a growing but carefully planned community with an emphasis on "green" building and sustainable design.

Of the 1,600 acres it occupied, 900 acres—more than half—had been preserved, in perpetuity, as forestland and open space, through which 24 miles of biking and hiking trails now ran.

Rita's message—that newness and old beauty can live together—had definitely gotten out.

I could see it in her life. I could see it in the success of her artwork and the college that she had started. I could see it in her footprint on the land around her.

And as my flight home lifted off the runway, I could hear it in her voice, still echoing in my psyche:

As you grow older, if you mature and your thinking is reasonable and rational, you can do anything you want. For me, at any rate, I will just go on doing. Because I cannot imagine giving up on what's still in my heart and in my mind.

This was, indeed, the kind of 80-year-old I someday want to be.

chapter eleven

The Encore Manifesto

Leveraging the Age Wave

Every generation needs a new revolution.
—Thomas Jefferson

Not long after beginning to write this book, I came to discover, in a corner of central San Francisco flush with investment banks, law firms, and luxury hotels, an enterprise of a different kind.

Part social movement, part philanthropy, part support group, this organization's mission was to construct—perhaps "conjure up" is a better way to put it—a brand new stage of life.

Manning the corner office was founder and CEO Marc Freedman, a charming, loquacious early 50-something with a big grin and a seemingly primal urge for change.

To Marc's way of thinking, the fact that tens of millions of Americans had entered their forties, fifties, and sixties with unprecedented life expectancies of 80 years or more meant that the need for a huge social tipping point was present and clear:

The idea of the 30-year retirement is simply unsustainable. Who can afford to retire for 30 years, and what society can afford to write off the most experienced quarter of its population when they still have so much left to contribute? We need a new map of life. And that's why now we're going to need to create a new category between midlife and old age.[1]

At the heart of Marc's vision was a magnetically simple idea: a new "graduate" career track. One that would allow people in midlife and beyond who find themselves unemployed, burned out at work, or retired and bored, to slide over into new jobs in the social sector that would provide them with "passion, purpose, and a paycheck" while solving some of society's biggest challenges.

Quite surprisingly, he told me, the idea first struck him while he was struggling through his first years of college:

I came out of a Philadelphia high school of 6,000 students where very little learning occurred, and I found myself a scholarship student at Swarthmore, a small college where I was really in over my head. The way things worked out, I went to see one of the deans there who was sort of entrusted with students who were struggling. He was in his late sixties at the time, and he had an indelible influence on me—you could say he changed my life.

From that time forward, Marc—who graduated with honors and went on to earn an MBA degree from Yale—was smitten with the notion that older men and women made up a "deep repository of life experience" that could be leveraged to mentor not only individuals but the nation and world.

As he made his way through early adulthood, he became increasingly certain of this idea and determined to convince others that it was so. To accomplish this, he began honing a three-pronged approach: First, raise money. Second, gather smart, like-minded people. Third, *start talking* until society-at-large catches on.

An effective strategy or wishful thinking? It's hard to say. At times, Marc's formula produced remarkable results.

In his early twenties, while employed as a junior staffer at a nonprofit, Marc was assigned a $50,000 grant to start up an intergenerational social program. While such a bequest was tiny, by the usual standards, it was more than enough to give him a jump start:

> *I was this 24-year-old in the office, and they needed somebody to work on this project. So I started looking at this question of older people as mentors, and in the process I became enraptured with the foster grandparent program, this gem that had been created during the 1960s to match older people with young people as part of the war on poverty. I started thinking about a modernization of that program. And along with that, I wrote a paper about the role older people could play in developing younger people, which led to a presentation I was to deliver at a conference in Washington, D.C.*

At that conference, the keynote speaker was legendary social pioneer John W. Gardner, who was in his eighties at the time. Decades before, Gardner had headed the Carnegie Corporation, and then, as secretary of health, education and welfare, he had served as the architect of President Lyndon Johnson's Great Society reforms, including the foster grandparents program.

About an hour after Gardner's speech, Marc recalled:

I was walking down one end of this corridor, and he was coming toward me. I normally would not have accosted him, but for some reason on that particular day I did, and I started to tell him about the paper I had written. He was headed out because of a snowstorm, but he listened and then fished a paper of his own out of his briefcase, gave it to me, and took off. And that was kind of it. I really had to badger him for about a year after that.

This badgering eventually led to a close relationship between the two men and, in the mid-1990s, to a collaborative effort called the Experience Corps, which was initially a pilot project that dispatched 55-plus-year-old volunteers, some earning a small stipend, to tutor, mentor, and provide individual support to inner city elementary schoolchildren.

With guidance and encouragement from Gardner, and millions in start-up money that came through Gardner's longtime connections at several of America's largest philanthropies, Marc, in his late thirties, was able to launch his own nonprofit, Civic Ventures, which proceeded to grow the Experience Corps into a successful nationwide program, operating in 20 cities with several thousand volunteers.

But he discovered, in the process, that the kind of program he had built was hardly big, or ambitious, enough.

A New Stage of Work

Interested in spreading the word about the Experience Corps, Marc made a visit to New York several years after Civic Ventures got off the ground.

There he met with Ruth Wooden, one of the first women to shatter the glass ceiling and rise through the ranks of the male-dominated advertising industry. She had been a senior vice president and managing director at the international ad agency N.W. Ayer, and she was now the first female president of the Advertising Council, the nation's leading producer of public service campaigns.

Having recently entered her fifties, Ruth was instantly intrigued by Marc's work, both on a professional and personal level:

> *I'd been at the Ad Council for 10 years, and the thought of staying there another 10 or 15 years was just not viable in my head. I had already done everything I wanted to do there, and also I was at a unique point in my life because I was divorced and I had a 13-year-old child—a really bad combination, a 50-year-old mother and a 13-year-old child. A lot of hormones going in and out. So I was very much in a percolating mode, like what do I wanna do next?*
>
> *Remember, I worked in advertising, where most people get out at 60, at the latest. You're over 60, you have to be the CEO. So there were a lot of people that I knew in my circle that were looking at a lot of years ahead, and struggling with what to do with their lives.*

As a market research expert, Ruth also began to instinctively sense that the uncertainties that she and her colleagues were experiencing were part of a much broader phenomenon:

> *I had done a lot of work on baby boomers as a marketing force, and as it turns out, I am a proverbial canary in the*

mine for baby boomers, having been born in 1946 myself. I had learned throughout my career that being such a canary in the mine gave me a kind of head start in being able to predict various trends and interests. I could tell what was going to be hot in a few years because it was something I was thinking about. It's not that I'm so insightful; it's just that it was demographics.

And the demographics, of course, were huge: nearly 80 million baby boomers—the largest, most highly educated, career-oriented generation in history—had begun navigating middle age and the years beyond. How were they going to live? What were they looking for in this stage of life?

Ruth soon joined the board of Marc's organization, Civic Ventures, and she helped to initiate a series of in-depth studies to answer such questions:

And like a lot of movements, you look at what I would call the "leading edge." We were hearing a lot of "Oh, my God, I don't want to play golf for 10 years," as people were beginning to get a sense of this new longevity, the likelihood that their lives were going to be a lot longer than previous generations.

As Marc [Freedman] would say, the first people who went to Sun City were the leading edge of the "retirement as leisure model," but now you had this kind of leading edge of the baby boom saying, "Geez, that's not for me. I want to keep working. I don't want to work the way I've always done, but I want to work." And we started hearing a lot of, "I want to work at something else."

Over time, Ruth, Marc, and the Civic Ventures board, composed of people in the second half of their own lives, came to realize that their research was uncovering an unprecedented social sea change.

For most career people, through many decades, the prevailing mantra had been to "work, work, then retire and kick back as young as possible."

But with the extension of life expectancy, the fact that baby boomers constituted the first modern generation of knowledge workers, and thus possessed long-term intellectual potential, and the reality that, for millions, continuing to earn a living could be an economic imperative, the American dream had begun to change.

In growing numbers, people no longer envisioned themselves retiring, playing golf or bridge, and volunteering a few hours a week. Instead, in midlife and beyond, they wanted work that paid real money and made a meaningful difference.

This big swing in national mindset, Ruth advised, called for a commensurate repositioning at Civic Ventures:

> We had started out pretty much on a national service model—volunteering and that sort of thing. But at some point during a board meeting, as Marc will tell you, I said: "It's not just a new stage of life we're looking at. It's a new stage of work." And that's when we got started thinking about how to put a name on this concept, which we ultimately called an encore career.
>
> We realized that the real mission of Civic Ventures was to use the longevity revolution in service of solving social problems. Health care, environmental issues, education, youth

development—these are all huge problems that need human talent to address them, and here we were discovering a workforce kind of primed to do that.

But, she added, while the supply of potential encore careerists was building, uncertainty was building as well:

Whether the demand side, in other words, employers with matching jobs to offer, would bring the supply in—that's always been the hard question for us. You know, what prevents this from happening on a large scale?

Birth of the Encore Brand

Over the next half dozen years, Civic Ventures reinvented itself as a "think tank on boomers, work, and social purpose." With a growing infusion of funds from philanthropic powerhouses like the Atlantic Philanthropies and the John Templeton, Hewlett-Packard, and MetLife Foundations, a sophisticated PR and advocacy campaign was launched.

Its central message: the first millions of baby boomers would soon turn 60, with 50- and 40-somethings right behind. Even while winding down their primary careers, they were determined to continue working and could offer an unprecedented "experience dividend" to social sector organizations wise enough to hire them.

"Take Advantage of Us" opined Marc, in journals, white papers, and opinion columns in some of the nation's leading newspapers. "It will take more than the chance to stuff envelopes to capture the imagination of the coming wave of boomers."[2]

Surveys by Civic Ventures began to show a burgeoning positive response on the supply side of the equation—millions of older and younger boomers were attracted to the idea of "shifting toward good work" by moving into second careers in fields such as "education, health care, government, and social services."[3]

But on the demand side, Marc and his colleagues lamented, "doors are not opening. There is as yet little evidence of receptivity by the nonprofit sector in tapping this coming population. Indeed, . . . indifference toward the contribution of this group is often the prevailing perspective of these organizations. All dressed up, but where to go?"

In 2006, Civic Ventures upped the ante, hiring a powerful asset, Jim Emerman, previously chief operating officer at the American Society of Aging. Jim's mission was to create and direct an unparalleled new effort, the annual Purpose Prize, designed to spotlight the accomplishments of successful 60-plus-year-old social entrepreneurs and, by extension, the skills and know-how that mature workers could bring to society at large.

In the first few years of the program, Civic Ventures awarded nearly $2 million to people who had started a wide range of nonprofits of their own to tackle community and national problems.

Almost immediately, the Purpose Prize generated significant media coverage, elevating Civic Venture's profile and message: America's coming age wave was an advantage to be leveraged—not, as many had espoused, an increasing liability and danger.

A new book by Marc further underscored this point and served as a branding iron for the concept he had long envisioned. The pages of *Encore: Finding Work That Matters in the Second Half of Life*, declared: "Retirement as we know it is in the midst of being displaced as the central institution of the second half of life," and it foresaw a national movement "built around the dream of an encore career, at the intersection of income, new meaning, and significant contribution."[4]

But, Marc added, "boomers embarking on an encore career should not assume smooth sailing. Employers, generally, aren't helping."

Soon, this proved to be an understatement of inestimable proportions.

A Perfect Storm of Impacts

Triggered by the subprime mortgage crisis and the bursting of the U.S. housing bubble, starting in 2008, stock and credit markets quivered and collapsed, plunging the United States and other national economies into the broadest and deepest financial quagmire since the Great Depression.

Over time, some 8.5 million Americans lost their jobs in the (nonfarm) private sector, and the rate of unemployment among post-midlife workers more than doubled, to the highest level in at least 60 years. Barely midway in the downturn, employment-related age discrimination complaints had spiked some 30 percent.[5]

In the social sector, the recession crippled the budgets of many nonprofits and government agencies—the primary potential employers, as Civic Ventures saw it, for boomers seeking encore careers. Human services nonprofits, especially, were hit with a "triple whammy," according to Elizabeth Boris, director of the National Center for Charitable Statistics: donations went down and government funding dropped, while at the same time demand for services from these organizations escalated.[6]

"Guess what's expendable in nonprofit organizations?" Boris asked during a speech at the Clinton School of Public Service.

She already had the answer in hand.

In 2009, the second full year of what was now known as the Great Recession, data showed that, nationally, 38 percent of human services nonprofits had cut their staffs, 50 percent had frozen or reduced salaries, and more than 20 percent had been forced to cut programs, draw down on financial reserves, or borrow money, wherever they could. Some 42 percent ended the year with a deficit.[7]

Taken together, this amounted to the "perfect storm of impacts" on nonprofits, according to the Johns Hopkins Institute for Policy Studies.[8]

"Of more concern," said experts at the Urban Institute, "is the hollowing of organizational capacity that may take years to rebuild, if ever."[9]

Would all this portend an early, perhaps irreversible setback for the encore career movement? Or might it eventually lead to new opportunities in the social sector that maturing baby boomers could fill?

Adopting the latter perspective, Civic Ventures shifted into higher gear.

Raising the Decibel Level

While sending millions in grants to colleges that were training boomers for social purpose jobs and piloting a nonprofit fellowship program for post-midlife professionals, Marc recruited a group of strong, high-profile voices for the Civic Ventures chorus.

Among them was Marci Alboher, a former *New York Times* career columnist, whose assignment was to provide maturing boomers with encore career guidance—no easy challenge, she conceded, in the postrecessionary environment:

> We wouldn't be doing this if we thought there was an even match-up between interest in doing this kind of work and available opportunities. It's really hard right now to make an encore career happen. We're igniting a spark that we hope is contagious, so that people run with it.

Brought aboard also, as board members, were two leading players from an earlier social movement: Suzanne Braun Levine, founding editor of the groundbreaking feminist publication *Ms.* magazine, and Pulitzer Prize winner Ellen Goodman, who famously chronicled and helped shape the women's movement throughout her long newspaper career.

While acknowledging the barriers, both spoke optimistically about long-term prospects for an encore revolution.

Said Ellen:

> There's a real problem, as we all have acknowledged, on paid employment of older people. To turn around the language and to get that word encore careers out into the culture is pretty significant. I think that a lot of us who have been through the women's movement, if we have another movement in us—it has to be connected to aging. A lot of the culture would wish we'd shut up and stop examining our lives, but it's only natural that the generation that examined itself all the way through the life cycle is going to be examining this aging thing.

Suzanne told me:

All these social movements have been about the same things: the freedom to be who you can be, the need for social support systems, to get respect, all the same basic human rights. The other side of it is persuading the culture at large that this is going to be good for them too. I don't think the answer is going to be that the 58-year-old will be hired by the 43-year-old to do the job that the 40-year-old is now hired to do. But I think the structure can change. At the risk of sounding like an old feminist, there are other ways of operating that can be very productive.

In 2010, a study sponsored by Civic Ventures pointed to the possibility of more than 2 million future social sector job vacancies, should the right economic and labor force conditions emerge. "Those are all big ifs," responded an editor at the *Harvard Business Review*.[10] But at Stanford's Center on Longevity, director Laura Carstensen, another prominent new Civic Ventures board member, predicted that the doubters and naysayers would come to see the light:

I'm told by economists that there's a fixed pot of jobs—that's not true. That's what they said in the 1970s when women started entering the workforce. But what happened instead was that more jobs were created. The baby boomers are the best educated and healthiest group of older adults in human history. So that's a lot of talent in this pool, and I think people are going to need it, going to want it.

And what of the Civic Ventures pioneers?

In the years since first linking up with Marc Freedman and launching the encore campaign, Ruth Wooden had moved in and out of another high-profile position—the presidency of Public Agenda, the nonpartisan policy organization—and she had taken over as Civic Ventures chair of the board.

Although times and circumstances had shifted, she told me, Marc's original formula for social change still applied:

> *Make a lot of noise, create awareness, continue to be a thought leader, putting ideas out there. I liken it to block and tackle in football—it's really grind it out, stay on the ground, just keep going three yards forward, and every once in a while you get a chance for a long pass.*

And Marc himself, after running this gauntlet for more than a quarter century, accumulating 2 million frequent flyer miles along the way, marrying twice and fathering three children after age 45, while a bit more philosophical than when he started, was still hot on the trail:

> *I wonder how I'll wrestle with my kids without wrenching my back and how I'll pay college tuition in my seventies. The truth is, I will probably be working for another 25 years, the second half of my adult life.*[11]

Indeed, it would seem to come with the territory—creating a new stage of life, after all, can take a little time.

chapter
twelve

Realizing Your Potential

Lessons for Getting Started

Every man has his vocation. The talent is the call.
— Ralph Waldo Emerson

"My passion is solving puzzles," said Ken Wadland, sitting at home in Albion, Rhode Island.

"When I graduated from college, I found out that people would pay you a lot of money if you write computer programs that solve their puzzles. It worked out really well while the economy was doing well."

Then came the Great Recession of 2008 to 2009, when along with a pink slip, Ken's company assigned him the toughest puzzle of all: career obsolescence in his late fifties, much earlier than he could afford or had planned.

"At first I figured, do what they tell you to do: take your time, reassess your skills, restart your résumé."

But he soon came to realize that this would hardly be enough: "I'd been in the software industry my entire career.

When I looked around, I saw that I may never get another job; this may be it, I may be retired now. The problem for people like me is that what I did, not many people are looking for anymore."[1]

Down the eastern seaboard, in Washington, D.C., federal agencies are legally required to keep workers on the job regardless of their age. But the law doesn't specify *which* job, as Carol Morgan learned at age 55: "I had worked as a professional writer for the government my entire career. Suddenly, the job changed, the job description changed. I was given proofreading, essentially, and when I tried to get into other positions, I couldn't. I faced age discrimination at the Environmental Protection Agency, and it was done with no respect for me."

She toughed it out for another 10 years, but she finally quit: "I want to get paid where it doesn't matter, where it's strictly ability that counts."

Nine hundred miles further south, 58-year-old Joan Mc-Cleskey experienced a similar pain: in August of 2009, the subprime mortgage meltdown claimed her management career at TransCapital Bank in Fort Myers, Florida: "They came over, the president of the bank, the vice president, and told us they were shutting the branch in 90 days. The branch was doing great, but people in the company had made bad loans, so they needed to cut their costs. Why on earth did they let that happen?"

Eighteen months later, the unemployment checks stopped: "Most everything I'd saved up to that point, I've had to pay bills with, so the savings are not there. I've been without health insurance because the plans are too high. This is not what I expected at this time of my life. I've always been a very good, loyal employee, and I thought that's what everybody wanted when they hired people. Now I've found out that it's not. They want somebody that's younger, that will accept a lot less money."

Will employers ever embrace people in midlife and beyond?

Will the time come:

> When professionals like Ken Wadland, Carol Morgan, and Joan McCleskey aren't routinely dead-ended by economics or age discrimination?
>
> When the job market fully values long-term experience?
>
> When a new encore career track will truly be commonplace?
>
> When there are ready-made opportunities for career reinvention or extension, in life's new, much longer second half?

Perhaps.

But, as we've seen throughout this book, the successfully reinvented people I met, studied, and interviewed were unwilling to wait and see.

While their professional backgrounds differed widely—Shep Nuland the surgeon, Horace Deets the association executive, Marion Rosen the physical therapist, Gil Garcetti the attorney, Rita Spina the psychologist—each faced a similar crisis: career loss, burnout, or premature retirement in their fifties or early sixties.

And as told in their stories, all responded in the same way: they turned their breakdowns into opportunities to identify areas and interests that fascinated them; they explored how to leverage those fascinations into new work; and they envisioned ways to turn this work into new success.

In life's second half, they *designed* their reinventions—and then they *realized* them in the world. Each established a *personal entrepreneurship*, a viable structure that allowed them to profit financially, emotionally, cognitively, and physically, and over the long term—into their seventies, eighties, and, in some cases, nineties—from self-created work that they loved.

Do What You Love, the Money Will Follow

It's now more than three decades since the ancient Buddhist psychology of Right Livelihood—the plucky notion that innately inspired work is the ultimate source of personal happiness, self-development, and success—entered the American consciousness in a significant way.

It began in 1989, the year the term "white-collar recession" was initially coined to describe an ensuing economic downturn when, for the first time in U.S. history, highly educated professionals bore the brunt of massive corporate "downsizing," a euphemism also invented during this period.

What followed was a prolonged "jobless recovery" during which the writings of organizational psychologist Marsha Sinetar, a modern proponent of Right Livelihood, grew in popularity and influence.

Sinetar's book *Do What You Love, the Money Will Follow* served as a manifesto for millions of career men and women who were coming to realize that, in the new, knowledge-based, global economy, long-honored notions like corporate loyalty and job security had turned painfully passé.

Today, more than ever, her central message rings true, most especially for those of us in midlife and beyond:

▶ GIVEN THE REALITY OF CORPORATE, government, financial, and technological upheaval in the twenty-first century, our new job security requires healthy entrepreneurial prowess. We only gain lasting job security by getting our mind to move beyond the notion that someone *else* should give us a job, find it for us, or tell us what to do with our life.

To build the life you want—complete with inner satisfaction, personal meaning and rewards—*create* the work you love.[2]

Recounting her own career reinvention, from public high school teacher and principal to the head of her own successful corporate consultancy, Sinetar wrote: "The thought of letting go of what I had—a well-paying, secure job; a beautiful home; friends and family nearby—was truly terrifying. I could not even imagine how to start."[3]

Though she had no business connections or background, she persevered in discovering her own Right Livelihood and building a platform for its materialization: "I wanted to *create* my own work as I might a sculpture or weaving. I saw entrepreneurship as practical—not some abstract concept for business school graduates or venture capitalists. I knew that if I stayed faithful to my aspirations, I would create my own niche."[4]

And that she did, going on to advise some of America's leading corporative executives and to become an international bestselling author.

While the *Do What You Love* approach may at first sound "airy fairy," Sinetar was hardly a Pollyanna. She never suggested that working at what you love means doing what you *feel* like or that money will automatically follow when you "go with the flow."

If anything, her guidance was sober and pragmatic: success, she counseled, ultimately "rests in your ability to find a fit between what you *need* and what *others* want." And, she cautioned: "in some cases, people who embarked on finding, and doing, work they loved are still waiting for the money to follow. I maintain that hard, patient disciplined long-term effort is required to do one's right livelihood."[5]

This kind of disciplined effort was a hallmark of every reinventive person I met while writing this book. Starting out, none had a small business background, and each faced the necessity of building a successful niche in the marketplace of people, products, and ideas before their personal potentials were realized.

Before their entrepreneurships got off the ground, and the money followed, there were lessons—sometimes hard ones—learned.

Lesson 1. Find Your Niche and Sell It

In her late fifties, veteran nurse-midwife Sharon Rising, a Yale nursing school graduate, became increasingly frustrated with the way things were going in her field and progressively fascinated with an idea for improving them.

In the Waterbury, Connecticut, hospital where she practiced, pregnant women frequently waited long hours for their appointments. When Sharon finally saw them, she had to rush through their exams to get to her next patient:

I was doing eight new ob/gyn intakes in a day, saying the same thing over and over and feeling like a tape machine. It was very clear to me that I was not going to be able to continue doing this, so I really needed to do something to save myself.

And I started thinking: What's private about being pregnant? Babies all grow in the same way. There's so much more to health care than a checkup, but we don't have time to teach people what they really need to know. Why don't we try prenatal care where patients come as a group and share their experiences with each other as well as their health-care provider?

For Sharon, group pregnancy care was a natural solution, and providing it felt like her personal Right Livelihood—work that she could love, use to serve others, and profit from as well. "I had a vision of a whole different kind of health-care paradigm," she told me. "I realized there was a much better way to give and receive prenatal care."

But others in the medical community, especially local physicians, were not convinced: What if the group process proved ineffective? What if complications resulted? What if they got sued? "It was not an easy time for me psychologically," Sharon recalled. "There was no support. I was working with obstetricians who had a whole different take on what care should be like."

Out of this initial resistance, Sharon learned a critical lesson in personal entrepreneurship: once you've found your niche, others must be sold on it too.

Upon recognizing this, she made it her priority:

At first, I presented the idea tentatively: I said, let's do three groups and evaluate it. And by the time the third group got started, the nurses came to me and said: "We have more women registering, but we don't have another group to put them in." I said, so what you're telling me is that you like the model? And they said, "Yes, absolutely."

From that, I found out how important it is to sell your ideas and make them really valuable to others by saying, "I've been looking at the way you've been doing things. You need me. This is the experience that I have, and this is what I can bring to you."

Five years after her initial pilot programs, she remained frustrated at the slow pace with which her idea was spreading beyond her immediate professional circle. She rented out a hotel meeting room and offered to train other health-care professionals in her process:

At the time, I didn't have a business bone in me. Our family was personally footing a lot of this, and my goal was to somehow come out even. I really didn't think about the cost. I just had to do it. I said during those days, "Someday we'll look back on all this and say, 'Remember when we were making workbooks at home and going to Costco to get the binders?'"

But here to my first workshop came 26 or 27 people, and I was like, well, would you believe it? They were midwives, some nurses, and one physician, and I had said to others, "There is no doctor who I had believed would ever do this, because I couldn't imagine any physician sitting in a group for an hour and being quiet."

Meanwhile, people were starting to hear about it, and I did a workshop in the Bay Area, and one in Chicago and one in

New Haven. And so it started to spread. By getting out there and pushing the idea, I found a way to persuade people that the method really worked.

Over time, Sharon's programs were studied, written up in numerous medical journals, and recognized by the Mayo Clinic as important innovations in health-care delivery. A major university-based random control trial showed that her group-care approach resulted in a 33 percent reduction in preterm births over traditional one-on-one prenatal care and that patient satisfaction ratings were markedly higher.

In her mid-seventies, when I interviewed her, Sharon was continuing to spread her work, as president and CEO of the Centering Health Care Institute, the thriving organization she founded in 2001. Her institute provided group health-care training to medical professionals and oversaw a network of more than 60 affiliated centers nationwide.

Lesson 2. Stay Solvent and Focused

After a three-decade career in the news and information business, Mark Miller finally jumped the corporate track.

By his early fifties, he'd been through 10 years of job volatility, working at three different organizations, two of which were blue chip companies that subsequently hit the rocks. By the time the plug got pulled on his next job as editor at a major Chicago newspaper, he was ready to go off on his own:

I had this thought about information for the boomer generation, and I had worked on a big project related to that. It was a big market, an emerging market that's going to be growing for the next 20 years, and it has a huge information need. So that's where I decided to focus my efforts.

At first, he planned to work on boomer-related projects as an independent consultant to big media operations. He later decided to pursue his first love: doing journalism on his own.

Combining his expertise in financial reporting with his background in print and online technology, he started a one-man multimedia enterprise providing news and analysis on money matters of special importance to 50-plus-year-olds, and he authored a highly useful book on the topic: *The Hard Times Guide to Retirement Security.*

What he learned in the process, Mark told me, he regularly passes along:

> *There's an illusion of safety that people have when they have full-time jobs. A sense of comfort that, I think we've seen, is increasingly an illusion. Older workers are especially vulnerable to this. But when you decide to go on your own, you need to deal with the obvious fact that you can't count on a paycheck.*
>
> *The number one thing is that you need to cover your living expenses because you're looking to build a business that lets you earn a living and hopefully do even better than that. I'd say you need a minimum of six months of living expenses to carry you through that prerevenue period. There's no magic to that number—you might need more—it's just a rule of thumb.*
>
> *Number two is creating your identity, which is coming up with a company name, with whatever corporate structure you choose, and then the branding around that—so a website,*

stationery, that sort of thing. Also there's technology like high-speed Internet and phones and whatever insurance, travel, and entertainment expenses you need to get your business up and running.

Unlike large businesses start-ups, most small or solo entre-preneurships can likely be booted up, by Mark's estimation, for less than $10,000. And while they need not be built around a fancy or detailed business plan, establishing a clear focus from the get-go is critical to success:

I think the most important thing to think about is to really concentrate hard on what is your product or service and where, or whether, there's a need for it. I think a lot of other things can be figured out on the fly. For a lot of people, particularly if they're bouncing off a corporate layoff, sometimes the decision-making process can be kind of knee-jerk and re-flexive, rather than really thoughtful, analytical, or creative. It's kind of "I can keep doing what I was doing, but I'm just gonna do it on my own," or something not well thought out.

I don't think there's anything wrong with a little trial and error, as long as you can fund it, through savings, or through some initial revenue, and then transition to another type of income. The tricky part is not to get so diffuse in your focus that you screw up. It's a struggle because, particularly in the early days, there's a temptation to want to take any business that comes through the door, for understandable reasons. But if you're not careful, you don't have any coherent focus. Let your business judiciously evolve, as evidence warrants, but try not to be all over the place.

Does it make sense to hedge your bets by job hunting while simultaneously working for yourself? Based on personal experience and start-ups he has studied, Mark strongly advises against the idea:

> *If you're going to make a decision to develop a business, don't be sending out your résumé at the same time. First, you don't want to send mixed signals to the market. Second, it will diffuse your energy so that you will succeed at neither effort.*

While failure must be averted, so too can the road to personal entrepreneurship appear in the most unlikely places and ways.

Lesson 3. Expect the Unexpected

A decade after retiring from the cosmetics and beauty industry, where he'd been a sales and general manager at top firms like Fabergé, Yves Saint Laurent, and Lanvin, 65-year-old Mark Goldsmith was climbing the walls in his Manhattan apartment building—almost literally.

A veteran of three New York City marathons, he'd already tried commodity trading and business consulting in an effort to fill his time; in neither case were the challenges, or rewards, big enough:

> *I said to my wife, I'm earning $3,000 a day, and I'm working two days a year. This is not so terrific. And she said to me, "Why don't you volunteer?" And I said, "Yeah, at what?"*
>
> *Well, they have this program called Principal for the Day, where people go into the NYC school system once a year and*

they meet the students and they can give a lecture, or what-
ever they want, to let them know that society cares.

I'm a bit of a wise guy, so I asked for a tough school. And I
thought I was headed for the South Bronx or something, but
instead they asked me: Would I go to jail? And I said okay. So,
off to the famous Rikers Island I went, where 14,000 inmates
sleep every night. It turned out that Rikers has two schools,
one for adolescents, and one for older young men, mostly drug
pushers. My picking that school was an absolute lark.

What happened once he was behind bars? This successful
businessman felt an uncanny connection with the prisoners, and
they felt a bond with him:

What we had in common was that, at age 18 or 19, I had no
idea what I wanted to do with my life. I didn't have a clue. So
I knew the feeling of what it is to be directionless.

They had gotten a bad deal. They had come from broken
homes, broken communities, awful schools, and here they
were deciding to get their high school diplomas. So the mes-
sage from me, this guy in a suit, was that there's another fu-
ture out there besides selling drugs. And if they got themselves
some education and took some positive steps, you can never
tell what might happen.

The principal at Rikers Island was happy to have him back
often. But Mark eventually came to believe that his students
needed more than education while they were in prison—they
needed help to stay out, once they were released.

He began meeting and mentoring Rikers "alumni" at a Starbucks on Madison Avenue and Thirty-Ninth Street. "I drank more café lattes in one year," he told me, "than you can possibly imagine."

By chance, serendipity, synchronicity—call it what you will—Mark, then in his late sixties, had discovered his fascination, his Right Livelihood. But what to do with it next?

Like his initial stroke of luck, his answer seemed to come from the blue:

> We were on vacation, my wife and I and two other couples, on the southwest coast of Florida. And this woman we were with looked at me and said, "You know, you're the perfect candidate. Why don't you start your own nonprofit?" My wife has a doctorate in social work and had been in the not-for-profit world for years, but as a business guy, I had always mocked it: What's this namby-pamby not-for-profit stuff?
>
> At that point, I had been working out at Rikers and Starbucks for some time, but the actual thought of starting my own nonprofit, to give it some structure and bring in other people to help, had never entered my mind. And I figured, why not? I've got management experience, and I've been raising money my whole life.

When I spoke with Mark, shortly after his seventy-fourth birthday, his nonprofit organization Getting Out and Staying Out, with six full-time employees and a cadre of volunteers, had provided more than 1,500 Rikers Island graduates with job-hunting, housing, and financial assistance. More than 80 percent, twice the usual average, had stayed out of prison. Most were working or pursuing college degrees; many were doing both at the same time.

He had garnered support from some of America's leading foundations, been honored by New York's mayor Michael Bloomberg, and been selected by Civic Ventures as a recipient of its $100,000 national Purpose Prize.

And what, I asked, did he—should we—gather from all this?

It was pure serendipity that my wife told me to go and be principal for a day. If not, I never would have stepped foot in a jail. It was happenstance to have a friend suggest I start a nonprofit. And I really lucked out again because my wife knew all the guidelines.

After that, it's been my willingness to work at it, to make it happen, one way or the other. If you find a passion or direction, you have to get out there and try something. After you think about it, then go out and begin.

As I tell young people: You just never know how things may work out.

The Rhythm of Reinvention

After Michelangelo died,
someone found in his studio a piece of paper
on which he had written a note to his apprentice, in
the handwriting of his old age:
Draw, Antonio, draw, Antonio,
draw and do not waste time.
—Annie Dillard, *The Writer's Life*

I t's axiomatic that human organizations—nations, governments, industries, businesses, political parties, communities, and schools, to name a few—must be willing to reinvent themselves in order to flourish over time.

As I write this, the descendants of ancient Egyptians are filling the streets of Cairo, seeking to sweep away the old order, to install a new government in the place of a 30-year-old regime.

In the boardroom of a large, established British corporation with which I collaborate as a leadership consultant, a new president—this company's first female senior executive—is working to dramatically reorganize its structure, for the purpose of remaining competitive in an ever-shifting global market.

Across America, cities are rebuilding and revitalizing their inner cores and infrastructures, lest they wither and die. Universities are revising their curricula to ensure that their graduates will be ready for the future.

While it may be messy and uncertain, we know instinctively that there is power in reinventing our institutions, that this is the best way to actualize their promise; we celebrate a headline that reads "Team Reinvents Itself" because it means that something positive has begun.

And yet, when we hit a certain stage in our own chronology, we tend to pull in our horizons—unconsciously buying into outdated stereotypes, we underestimate the long-term potential within ourselves.

"At this age," many of us say, "the most I can expect to earn, achieve, experience is . . ."

In the past century, the human lifespan itself has been re-engineered—the additional decades given to us by science and medicine have never been lived by previous generations; they are essentially brand new.

Should not our assumptions about them be too?

As anthropologist Mary Catherine Bateson points out: "We have not added decades to life expectancy by simply extending old age; instead, we have opened up a new space part-way through the life course, a second and different kind of adulthood. Increased longevity will challenge us not only to revise expectations, but also to discover unexpected possibilities."[1]

I spent the better part of five years exploring these possibilities while researching and writing this book.

As happened frequently in my earlier career as a traveling news correspondent, even while I sought to chronicle my findings for you, my reader, I experienced a journey of great discovery for myself.

I organized this project around a series of questions that I had begun to wrestle with personally—questions that I was also hearing from others who had arrived, often to their surprise, in midlife or the years beyond:

After a career of 20, 30, or 40 years, am I a done deal?

**Is it true that success is necessarily
a younger person's game?**

**Is it possible to make money and a difference
in the decades to come?**

**Might there be more potential within each of us
than we've been led to believe?**

In the search for answers, I studied antiquity, modern history, and contemporary affairs. I delved into philosophical, psychological, sociological, demographic, economic, medical, and neuroscientific research at the cutting edge.

And, most importantly, I got to know a group of men and women in their sixties, seventies, eighties, and nineties who changed everything I had ever previously thought about the nature of getting older.

From their life experiences came my most valued discoveries.

Discovery 1

Beginning at age 45 or 50, you and I have undeveloped, even hidden potential—talents, skills, and forms of advanced intelligence that were not available to us in life's first half. As both human history and modern neuroscience have suggested, we seem to be hardwired for reinvention and continuing success.

Discovery 2

The highest level of human happiness — the flow experience — is accessed not by "kicking back" or reflecting on previous achievements but by identifying and putting our full lifetime potential to work.

Discovery 3

As we navigate midlife and the years beyond, each of us faces a choice. We can decide to "retire" our ambitions, to downshift our aspirations. Or we can choose to reinvent — to redirect our course, to pursue what happiness, profits, and purpose may yet be ours to find.

And this I discovered as well: there is a magic in the decision to unlock our potential — an inexplicable phenomenon that seems to trigger positive outcomes when we commit to the course. And there is an underlying rhythm, a life-affirming cadence that carries us through the process, if we're willing to take the first steps.

I once heard the Nobel poet laureate Seamus Heaney, then approaching the seventh decade of his own life, seek to describe this to young graduates in a college commencement address.

Now, having completed this book, I am certain — as I hope you are — that the rhythm he refers to awaits us at any age:

> *Getting started, keeping going, getting started again — in art and in life, it seems to me, this is the essential rhythm, not only of achievement but of survival — never resting upon the oars of success or in the doldrums of disappointment, but getting renewed and revived by some further transformation.*

You have reached a stepping stone in your life, a place where you can pause for a moment and enjoy the luxury of looking back on the distance covered.

But the thing about stepping stones is that you always need to find another one up there ahead of you.

Even if it is panicky in midstream, there is no going back.

Even if the last move did not succeed, the inner command says: move again.

There is no surefire do-it-yourself kit.

There is only risk and truth to yourself.

The world where we are to make our tarry mark lies before us.[2]

Notes

Chapter 1

1. www.efmoody.com/estate/lifeexpectancy.html.
2. Peter F. Drucker, *Management Challenges for the 21st Century*, HarperBusiness, New York, 1999, pp. 188–194.

Chapter 2

1. Sherwin B. Nuland, *How We Die*, Knopf, New York, 1993, p. 264.
2. Lisa Belkin, "The Senator Track," *New York Times Magazine*, January 14, 2009, p. 10.
3. Gene D. Cohen, MD, *American Journal of Geriatric Psychology*, February 1999, p. 1.
4. George E. Valliant, MD, *Aging Well*, Little, Brown, New York, 2002, pp. 40, 41.
5. Gene D. Cohen, MD, *The Mature Mind*, Thorndike Press, Detroit, 2005, p. 17.
6. Gene D. Cohen, MD, *The Creative Age*, Avon Books, New York, 2000, p. 77.
7. Betty Friedan, *The Fountain of Age*, Simon & Schuster, New York, 1993, p. 23.
8. Barry Gewen, Books of the Times, "A Doctor Finds Miracles in Medicine," *New York Times*, June 6, 2008.

Chapter 3

1. Peter F. Drucker, "Managing Oneself," *Harvard Business Review*, March–April 1999.
2. Hara Estroff Marano, "The Creative Self," *Psychology Today*, March 10, 2004.
3. Carol Hymowitz, "Ex-CEOs Look for Some Challenges in Their Second Acts," *Wall Street Journal*, September 10, 2007.
4. Joseph Campbell, *The Power of Myth*, Programs 1 through 6, audiocassettes, Apostrophe S. Productions, 1988. Also Joseph Campbell with Bill Moyers, *The Power of Myth*, Anchor, New York, 1991, pp. 118–148.
5. Ibid., Introduction, p. xiv.
6. Joan Konner, Huston Smith, Roy Finch, Carol Wallace Orr, Robert H. Markman, et al., "Joseph Campbell: An Exchange," *New York Review of Books*, vol. 36, no. 17, November 9, 1989.

7. David Hochman, Inspire Awards, 2010 Honorees, "Clint Eastwood: Daring Director," *AARP The Magazine*, January–February 2010, p. 64.
8. Dina Eastwood, "Clint Eastwood," *Artworks* magazine, March 18, 2008, p. 59.
9. Bill Gates, 2009 Annual Letter, www.gatesfoundation.org.
10. Dante Alighieri, *The Divine Comedy*, translated by John Ciardi, W.W. Norton, New York, 1977, p. 62.
11. William Bridges, *Transitions*, Addison-Wesley, Reading, Mass., 1980, pp. 18, 121.
12. Dava Sobel, Interview, Mihaly Csikszentmihalyi, *Omni Magazine*, January 1995.
13. Mihaly Csikszentmihalyi, *Finding Flow*, Basic Books, New York, 1997, p. 4.
14. Mihaly Csikszentmihalyi, *Flow*, Harper & Row, New York, 1990, p. 3.
15. *Encyclopedia of World Biography 2006*, Gale Group, www.encyclopedia.com.
16. David M. Halbfinger, "Jack Valenti, 85, Confidant of a President and Stars, Dies," *New York Times*, April 27, 2007.
17. Jeanine Basinger, Books of the Times, "Walking with Presidents and (Hollywood's) Kings," *New York Times*, June 26, 2007.
18. Mihaly Csikszentmihalyi, *Creativity*, HarperCollins, New York, 1996, pp. 207–208.
19. Extrapolated from Csikszentmihalyi, *Finding Flow*, *Flow*, and *Creativity*.
20. Csikszentmihalyi, *Flow*, p. 42.

Chapter 4

1. Phyllis Moen, Commentary, New Face of Work Survey, MetLife Foundation/Civic Ventures, San Francisco, 2005.
2. Ibid., pp. 2, 3, 57, 59.
3. David Corbett, *Portfolio Life*, Wiley, San Francisco, 2007, pp. 32–33.
4. Glenn Ruffenach, "The Retirement Lies We Tell Ourselves," *Wall Street Journal*, December 22, 2006, p. R4.
5. Society for Human Resource Management (SHRM), "Employers Lukewarm about Retaining Older Workers," May 21, 2007, www.shrm.org.
6. Julie Creswell and Karen Donovan, "Happy Birthday. Vacate Your Office," *New York Times*, December 8, 2006, pp. C1–C10; and Adam Cohen, Editorial, "After 40 Years, Age Discrimination Still Gets Second Class Treatment," *New York Times*, November 6, 2009.

7. Steve Lohr, "For a Good Retirement, Find Work, Good Luck," *New York Times*, June 22, 2008, p. WK3.
8. MetLife Mature Market Institute, "New Realities of the Job Market for Aging Baby Boomers," San Francisco, October 2009.
9. *The Shattered American Dream* report, John J. Heldrich Center for Workforce Development, December 2010, p. 17.
10. Report by Peter D. Hart Research Associates, MetLife Foundation/Civic Ventures Encore Career Survey, June 2008.
11. Report by Peter D. Hart Research Associates, June 2008 MetLife Foundation/Civic Ventures Survey of Nonprofit Employers, June 2008, pp. 35, 39.
12. Report by Barry Bluestone, Northeastern University, "After the Recovery: Help Needed—The Coming Labor Shortage and How People in Encore Careers Can Help Solve It," March 22, 2010, www.encore/org/research.
13. Jason Tanz with Theodore Spencer, "Candy Striper My Ass!" *Fortune*, August 14, 2000.
14. Marc Freedman, "Academics Pioneer the Third Age," *Chronicle of Higher Education*, April 29, 2005.
15. Robert Egger, Commentary, New Face of Work Survey, MetLife Foundation/Civic Ventures, San Francisco, 2005.
16. Civic Ventures, The Purpose Prize, News Release, December 3, 2008.
17. Stanford University Public Forum, September 7, 2006.

Chapter 5

1. Andrew D. Blechman, *Leisureville: Adventures in America's Retirement Utopias*, Atlantic Monthly Press, New York, 2008, p. 15.
2. Ibid., p. 17.
3. Ibid., p. 13.
4. John Leland, quoting Andrew D. Blechman in "Using It before Losing It," *New York Times Sunday Book Review*, June 1, 2008, p. 48.
5. Marc Freedman, *Prime Time*, PublicAffairs, Cambridge, Mass., 2002, p. 22.
6. Thomas R. Cole, *The Journey of Life*, Cambridge University Press, New York, 1992, pp. 212–221.
7. Ibid., p. 216.
8. Joanna Short, "Economic History of Retirement in the United States," Economic History Association, www.EH.net, posted February 2010.
9. *Time*, "A Place in the Sun," cover story, August 3, 1962.

10. U.S. Bureau of Labor Statistics.
11. U.S. Census Bureau, CB99-FF.17, December 20, 1999.
12. *Time*, "A Place in the Sun."
13. www.pulte.com.
14. Freedman, *Prime Time*, p. 40, and Freedman, "The Selling of Retirement," *Washington Post*, February 6, 2005.
15. Marc Freedman, *Encore*, PublicAffairs, Cambridge, Mass., 2007, p. 52.

Chapter 6

1. Marion Rosen and Susan Brenner, *Rosen Method Bodywork*, North Atlantic Books, Berkeley, Calif., 2003, p. 1.
2. Ibid, p. 3.
3. Ibid, p. 7.

Chapter 7

1. Abby Ellin, "Preludes: When a Buddy Makes It Big," *New York Times*, February 21, 1999.
2. Stanford Graduate School of Business, "A Closer Look: Steve Aldrich MBA 1995," *Stanford Business Bulletin*, March 1999.
3. Elkhonon Goldberg, PhD, *The Wisdom Paradox*, Gotham Books, New York, 2005, pp. 48, 52.
4. Richard Restak, MD, *Older and Wiser*, Simon & Schuster, New York, 2007, p. 238.
5. Goldberg, *The Wisdom Paradox*, p. 48.
6. Tom Long, "Anna Morgan, at 101; Was Active in Labor, Civil Rights Movement," *Boston Globe*, August 3, 1996, encyclopedia.com.
7. John Robbins, *Healthy at 100*, Thorndike Press, Waterville, Me., 2006, pp. 368–371.
8. Philip J. Hilts, "Life at 100 Is Surprisingly Healthy," *New York Times*, June 1, 1999.
9. Robbins, *Healthy at 100*, pp. 371–372.
10. Merzenich blog, July 13, 2009, www.merzenich.positscience.com.
11. Norman Doidge, *The Brain That Changes Itself*, Penguin, New York, 2007, p. 61.
12. Ibid., pp. 47–49.
13. Ibid., p. 87.
14. Geoff Colvin, *Talent Is Overrated*, Penguin, New York, 2008, pp. 180–184.

15. Betty Friedan, *The Fountain of Age*, Simon & Schuster, New York, 1993, pp. 217–218.
16. Stephen S. Hall, "The Older & Wiser Hypothesis," *New York Times Magazine*, May 6, 2007, p. 60.
17. Gene D. Cohen, *The Creative Age*, Avon Books, New York, 2000, p. 60.
18. *60 Minutes* interview with Chesley Sullenberger, February 8, 2009, cbsnews.com.
19. Alex Altman, "Chesley B. Sullenberger III Profile," *Time*, February 16, 2009, time.com.
20. Bill Newcott, "Wisdom of the Elders," *AARP The Magazine*, May-June 2009, p. 52.
21. Goldberg, *The Wisdom Paradox*, p. 20.
22. Ibid., p. 288.
23. Ibid., p. 13.
24. Brett Wilbur, "A Gratifying Ride," *Carmel Magazine*, Winter 2009.
25. Carla Hay, "Clint Eastwood Reveals," *San Francisco Examiner*, June 10, 2009, www.examiner.com.
26. Hall, "The Older and Wiser Hypothesis," p. 64.
27. Beth Levine, "The Happiness Equation," *Woman's Day*, August 2008, womansday.com.
28. Duke Medicine News, "Old and Young Brains Rely on Different Systems to Remember Emotional Content," December 16, 2008, DukeHealth.org.

Chapter 8

1. *CBS News Sunday Morning*, May 26, 2006.
2. Sara Terry, "Gil Garcetti Prosecutes a New Cause: Shooting Photos That Make a Difference," *Christian Science Monitor*, October 18, 2007

Chapter 9

1. Mortimer J. Adler, Speech to the National Association of Life Under-writers, July 16, 1962, and article in the *Journal of the American Society of Life Underwriters*, Winter 1963. Excerpted with permission of the Adler archive.
2. Edith Hamilton, *The Greek Way*, W.W. Norton, New York, 1930, p. 15.
3. Ibid., p. 31.
4. Translations of excerpts from works by Homer, Aristotle, Plato, and others are based on a variety of sources, including Adler, speech to the

National Association of Life Underwriters, and Hamilton, *The Greek Way*.

5. Diane Harris-Cline, quoted in Brian Krause, "Tracing the Flow of the Greek Aesthetic," By George! Online, George Washington University News Center, October 15, 2002, www.gwu.edu.

6. Edith Hamilton, *The Echo of Greece*, W.W. Norton, New York, 1964, p. 30.

7. Menelaos L. Batrinos, "The Length of Life and Eugeria in Classical Greece," *Hormones* (Athens), vol. 7, no. 1, January–March 2008, pp. 82–83. U.S. National Library of Medicine, www.ncbi.nlm.nih.gov/pubmed/18359748.

8. Erik Erikson, "Insight and Responsibility" (1964)," *The Erik Erikson Reader*, W.W. Norton, New York, 2000, p. 205.

9. Ibid., p. 204.

10. Lawrence K. Altman, "The Doctor's World," *New York Times*, December 25, 2006.

11. Sherwin B. Nuland, *The Art of Aging*, Random House, New York, 2007, p. 65.

12. Ibid., pp. 68–74.

13. *Stanford Encyclopedia of Philosophy*, www.plato.stanford.edu.

14. David Brooks, "Nice Guys Finish First," *New York Times*, May 17, 2011.

15. Lara B. Aknin, Christopher P. Barrington-Leigh, Elizabeth W. Dunn, et al., *Prosocial Spending and Well-Being: Cross-Cultural Evidence for a Psychological Universal*, Harvard Business School Working Paper 11-038, October 27, 2010.

16. *Economicae: An illustrated Encyclopedia of Economics*, www.unc.edu/depts/econ.

17. Stewart Wills, interviewer, and Ulrich Mayr, interviewee, "Neurobiology of Charitable Giving," *Science* Magazine Podcast, June 15, 2007.

18. www.nih.gov/researchmatters/june2007.

19. R. Bowen, "Physiologic Effects of Oxytocin," last updated July 12, 2010, www.vivo.coloradostate.edu.

20. Richard P. Sloan, "A Fighting Spirit Won't Save Your Life," Op-Ed page, *New York Times*, January 25, 2011.

21. Stephanie L. Brown and R. Michael Brown, Letter to the Editor, *New York Times*, January 25, 2011.

22. Pam Pelluck, "Nuns Offer Clues to Alzheimer's and Aging," *New York Times*, May 7, 2001.

23. Sylvia McGill et al., "Experience Corps: Design of an Intergenerational Program to Boost Social Capital and Promote the Health of an Aging

Society," *Journal of Urban Health, Bulletin of the New York Academy of Medicine,* vol. 81, no. 1, March 2004, pp. 94–105.

24. Stephen G. Post, *The Hidden Gifts of Helping,* Wiley/Jossey-Bass, San Francisco, 2011, as quoted in the excerpt of this book posted on the Noetic Now blog, April 2011, www.noetic.org/noetic/issue-nine-april/hidden-gifts/.

Chapter 11

1. Glenn Hodges, "Interview with Marc Freedman on the Midlife Crisis," *AARP Bulletin,* May 12, 2011.

2. Marc Freedman, "Take Advantage of Us," *Stanford Social Innovation Review,* Fall 2004.

3. Marc Freedman, "The Boomers, Good Work, and the Next Stage of Life," New Face of Work Survey, MetLife Foundation/Civic Ventures, San Francisco, June 2005.

4. Marc Freedman, *Encore: Finding Meaningful Work in the Second Half of Life,* PublicAffairs, Cambridge, Mass., 2007, pp. 11, 20, 88.

5. Richard W. Johnson and Janice Park, "Can Unemployed Older Workers Find Work?" Urban Institute, January 12, 2011, www.urban.org; and Michael Luo, "Longer Periods of Unemployment for Workers 45 and Older," *New York Times,* April 13, 2009.

6. Elizabeth Boris, "The Economic Recession and Nonprofits," speech at the Clinton School of Public Service, June 10, 2010, www.clintonschoolspeakers.com.

7. Elizabeth Boris, Erwin de Leon, Katie L. Roeger, and Milena Nikolova, Executive Summary, *Urban Institute National Survey of Nonprofit Government Contracting and Grants,* October 7, 2010, www.urban.org.

8. Lester M. Salamon, Stephanie L. Geller, and Kasey L. Spence, *Impact of the 2007–09 Recession on Nonprofit Organizations,* Johns Hopkins Center for Civil Society Studies, 2009, www.css.jhu.edu.

9. Boris, de Leon, Roeger, and Nikolova, Executive Summary, *Urban Institute National Survey of Nonprofit Government Contracting and Grants.*

10. Bronwyn Fryer, "Where the Boomers Will Find Jobs," HBR Blog Network, March 29, 2010, www.hbr.org.

11. Marc Freedman, *The Big Shift,* PublicAffairs, Cambridge, Mass., 2011, p. 5.

Chapter 12

1. *Stories of the Great Recession*, www.over50andoutofwork.com.
2. Marsha Sinetar, *To Build the Life You Want, Create the Work You Love*, St. Martin's Press, New York, 1995, pp. 3, 5.
3. Marsha Sinetar, *Do What You Love, the Money Will Follow*, Paulist Press, Mahwah, N.J., 1987, p. 1.
4. Sinetar, *To Build the Life You Want, Create the Work You Love*, pp. 9, 10.
5. Ibid., pp. 4, 17.

Epilogue

1. Mary Catherine Bateson, *Composing a Further Life*, Knopf, New York, 2010, pp. 12, 19.
2. Seamus Heaney, excerpt from a commencement address given to University of North Carolina at Chapel Hill graduates in a Kenan Stadium ceremony on May 12, 1996. Reprinted by personal permission of the author.

Acknowledgments

"When a writer is born into a family, that is the end of the family." So wrote Nobel laureate V. S. Naipaul.

Fortunately, that has been far from my experience. In fact, while researching and writing this book, I discovered that endeavors such as this one can not only tighten existing relationships but sprout new and wonderful connections as well.

For her tireless support of this project, I owe my wife and life partner, Jane, the sort of appreciation that cannot be expressed by words alone. When I cautioned her, at the outset, to expect elongated mental and physical absences on my part, she responded, as she has through the years, "You need to do what you need to do, to be who you are." Along with her ongoing encouragement and invaluable conceptual and editorial contributions, my greatest reward has been watching her apply the lessons and concepts in this book to her own life. She has become a truly reinventive woman.

I am also inestimably indebted to a group of remarkable people who generously allowed me to probe their personal and professional experiences, while also sharing their contacts with me, so that I might formulate and make this project a reality.

First among them is Horace Deets who, along with his unparalleled insights, example, and mentorship, connected me with Drs. Shep Nuland and Gene Cohen, whose contributions to my writing proved extraordinarily important. Sadly, Gene passed away while this book was still a work in progress. His spirit lives on in these pages.

I cannot thank enough the other "primary players" in the book who provided me with the real-life scripts around which it revolves: Rita K. Spina and Marion Rosen, both of whom felt like family from the moment we met, as well as Gil Garcetti, Mark Miller, Sharon Rising, and Mark Goldsmith, all of whom I am now gratified to call friends.

My deep appreciation extends also to the key subject experts who enthusiastically offered me the kind of informed and enlightened context that is essential for any serious journalistic undertaking: my longtime friend and fellow writer Mike Murphy, as well as my newfound comrades on the frontiers of life's second half, including Marc Freedman, Ruth Wooden, Jim Emerman, Marci Alboher, Suzanne Braun Levine, Ellen Goodman, Laura Carstensen, Steven Aldrich, and Elizabeth Pope.

My gratitude goes also to Bill Ury at Harvard, for his friendship, our brainstorming, and his support from the start of this project, and to Nobel laureate Seamus Heaney, who inspired me and so kindly allowed me to share his powerful words in these pages.

A note of particularly special thanks goes to my super agent, Cindy Zigmund at Second City Publishing Services. A veteran of decades in the publishing trenches, Cindy saw the power and potential of this project from day one and unwaveringly worked to mold it, improve it, and ultimately make it a reality by forging our alliance with the fine folks at McGraw-Hill.

There, I thank Leila Porteous, David Moldawer, Ron Martirano, Jane Palmieri, and the superb team of editorial, design, and business professionals who made it possible for *Boundless Potential* to find its way into your life.

A Life of Reinvention

Mark S. Walton is a Peabody Award–winning journalist, former CNN Senior Correspondent and anchor, Fortune 100 executive educator, and internationally acclaimed leadership consultant whose work at the highest levels of business, government, the military, and academia has spanned more than four decades.

In his early twenties, Mark served as a U.S. Navy officer assigned to a guided missile destroyer during the Vietnam War. Soon thereafter, he was assigned to the Pentagon, where he was a media advisor and spokesman for the Secretary of the Navy and the Chief of Naval Operations.

He was a founding correspondent of CNN at age 30 and, subsequently, one of America's most visible and accomplished television journalists. Hank Whittemore's book CNN: *The Inside Story* characterizes him as "part of a small gang of renegades who changed the face of TV news." His live coverage of major breaking news and in-depth reporting and analysis of domestic and global politics and social trends were awarded the news industry's premier honors, including the coveted Peabody Award, the National Headliner Award, the Ohio State Journalism Award, the Cable Ace Award, the Gold Medal of the New York TV and Film Festival, and the Silver Gavel of the American Bar Association.

Upon reinventing himself again in his forties, Mark was named a Professor of Leadership in the U.S. Navy's Advanced Management Program and a Distinguished Lecturer in management at the Senior Executive Institute and the nationally top-ranked Kenan-Flagler Business School at the University of North Carolina at Chapel Hill.

While on the Carolina faculty, he founded the Center for Leadership Communication, an executive education and development organization with a focus on leadership and exceptional achievement at every stage of life. Additionally, he authored *Generating Buy-In: Mastering the Language of Leadership*, which was published by the American Management Association in 2004 and selected by Soundview Executive Book Summaries as one of the top 30 business books of the year.

As chairman of the Center for Leadership Communication, Mark has appeared before, taught, coached, and advised tens of thousands of leaders, managers, and professionals in private consultations, graduate business schools, corporate and military universities, leadership training programs, management retreats, industry and association conferences, customized seminars, workshops, and public events worldwide.

To send him your thoughts and comments on this book, forward your own stories about career and personal reinvention, or arrange media interviews, speaking engagements, presentations, seminars, or workshops based on *Boundless Potential*, Mark can be contacted via e-mail to info@leadercommunication.com.

Index